SHIPPING INDUSTRIAL STRUCTURE

SHIPPING INDUSTRIAL STRUCTURE

LADI UTIEYIONE

Copyright © 2015 by Ladi Utieyione.

Library of Congress Control Number: 2015917414
ISBN: Hardcover 978-1-5144-1884-0
Softcover 978-1-5144-1883-3
eBook 978-1-5144-1882-6

All rights reserved. No part of this book may be reproduced or transmitted in any form or by any means, electronic or mechanical, including photocopying, recording, or by any information storage and retrieval system, without permission in writing from the copyright owner.

Print information available on the last page.

Rev. date: 04/25/2016

To order additional copies of this book, contact:
Xlibris
1-888-795-4274
www.Xlibris.com
Orders@Xlibris.com
724729

CONTENTS

Personnel and Organizations 1
Ship Interests 1
Cargo Interest 2
Ancillary Services 3
Flag 10
Registration 11
Jurisdiction 13
Flag State 13
Ship 14
Load Line 15
Tonnage 16
Crew 16
Minimum Standards (ILO 147) 16
STCW Convention 17
Crew Agreements 20
Environment 21
Other 22
COLREGS 1972 23
International Safety Management (ISM) Code 23
Structure of a Safety Management System 30
Port State Control 33

USCG Port State Control Initiative 37
Loan Security 46
The Future 46
Exercise: Ship Finance 47
Types of Maritime Trade 48
Cargo 49
Voyage Diagram 49
Liner Service 50
Liner Conferences (Conference Lines) 50
Tramp Operations 52
Passenger Ships 53
Other Cargoes 54
Contracts of Sale 69
Hague and Hague-Visby Rules 71
Hague-Visby Rules 71
Obligations under the HVRs 73
Deviation under the HVRs 79
Dangerous Goods under HVRs 80
Limitation of Liability 81
Special Agreements 82
Convention Countries 83
Demise Charter 87
Not by Demise 87
Time Charter Party 88
Clauses of Time Charter Party 90
Voyage Charter Party 95
Clauses of a Voyage Charter Party 97

Importance of Time and Cargo 109
Example 123
Exercise: Choice of Charter 125
Technical Aspects 129
Reports and Records 130
Expenditure Control 131
Reporting Incidents 131
Average 134
Marine Insurance 135
Insurance Procedure 136
Insurance Company 137
Lloyd's Syndicate 138
Captive Insurance 138
No Insurance 139
Insurance Policy 139
Institute Clauses 140
General Average 143
York-Antwerp Rules (1994) 143
General Average Adjustments 146
Shipowner's Liability 150
Claims for Liability 155
Oil Tankers 158
US Oil Pollution Act of 1990 (OPA) 160
Categories of Liens 162
Non-salvage Operations 173
Sample Note of Protest 175

ACKNOWLEDGMENT

I'm thankful to God who has giving me the Grace to put this piece of work together, I say a big thanks to my boss's, colleagues, my clients, my clubs, my friends, my associations, Government parastatals and my company team who has shared experiences with me on my career path. More especially I want to thank my wife and my lovely kids for their patients and support they showed me during the time I took in putting this piece of work together. It's been an amazing journey for me and everybody that has been in my life's path during this time.

Every author knows that writing a book is a team effort. Families sacrifice time together, publishing professionals work miracles, friends and associates are asked to review my work, validate ideas or perhaps even write something. My fellow industrial experts are contacted and asked to confirm their views, suggest additional references, and provide insight. I also read other books and conducted thorough research for needed references.

Thanks are due to many individuals, organizations and companies who made their information available to put this piece of work together. Protective and Indemnity Insurance clubs around the globe, case studies between companies, International Maritime Association, International Maritime Contractors, Classification Societies like LLOYDS, ABS, BV, DNV, RINA, etc. My fellow ship owners in Greece, Turkey, China, United Kingdom, United States of America, Africa, The Caribbean, Singapore, Russia, Japan, South Korea, Sweden, Denmark, Norway, Switzerland, Italy, Spain, India, and Australia.

My piece of work has been reviewed by some of the most respected individuals in the industry and the publishing company made it easy for me to publish it.

I am also grateful to you for reading this book.

PREFACE

Dealing effectively with requirements tops the list of the challenges to ship owners, cargo owners, regulatory bodies and auxiliary services in the marine industry. Improving and implementing professional services on ships and cargo practices has been my focus throughout my career. My vision in this book is to help individuals and companies maintain, improve and experience continual growth in their daily shipping operations. I have used common language shipping which enables anyone to understand shipping in a simple way.

My newly-released publication titled "Shipping Industrial Structure", is a book that highlights broad shipping and cargo practices. It clearly explains shipping complexity in a simple way for people outside the maritime industry who are interested in knowing the real meaning of shipping business and its norms.

In details, my book explains the interaction between a shipper, charterer, consignee, International marine regulatory bodies, shipping auxiliary services and all kinds of interests on ships, her cargos, and the people behind the scenes enforcing instructions to move vessels adherence to the rules and regulations that govern the industry. Shipping industrial structure demonstrates the process approach, complexities, port authorities, governmental laws and international certified organizations who take care of the shipping cycle operations worldwide.

Shipping industrial structure is designed for students and professionals within and out of the maritime industry. My book is designed for those who wants to understand the industry and how to approach businesses. It's a book that will give you a thousand idealistic approaches towards establishing your own maritime services.

This book serves as a guide to maritime attorneys, and other marine professionals who are engaged in ship operations and cases in different forms. It has reference points and solutions to issues surrounding the maritime industry. Little mistakes cost companies fortunes and they might never recover from such losses. In my opinion, it's usually good to have books for your workers and yourself to read. From my experience, incidents never tell you when they will come. The only way you can be prepared to tackle incidents is to read books and have as much information as possible.

Generally, this book is meant for professionals, schools, government officials, marine related crime investigators, and people from other industries.

1. Shipping Industrial Structure

| Shipper | Sea Carrier | Consignee |

The major component of the industry can be divided into three sections as follows

Shippers
Cargo Interest
Ancillary services

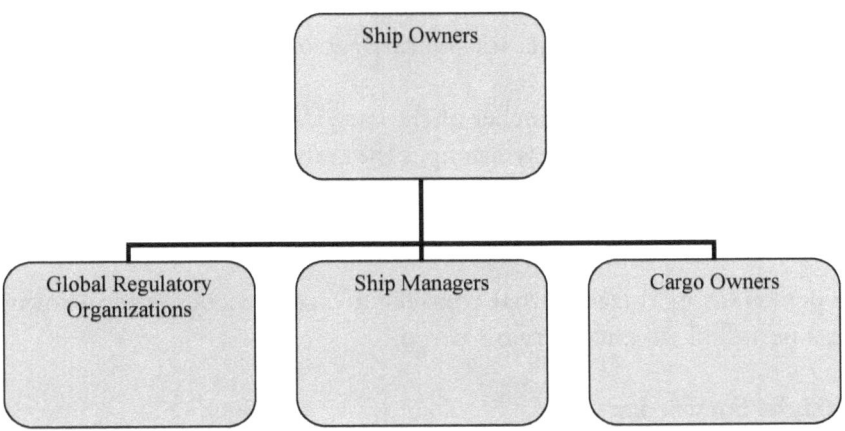

Ship Interest
Ship Manager
Shipping line
Carrier

Shipping Line

A company which operates a ship or ships between advertised ports on a regular basis and offers space for goods in return for freight based on a tariff of rates.

Carrier

The shipowner or charterer or whoever enters into a contract with the shipper for the transportation of merchandise.

Cargo Interest

- Shipper
- Charterer
- Freight forwarder

Shipper

A person or company who enters into a contract with a liner conference, shipping line, or shipowner for the carriage of goods.

The shipper could be the seller of the cargo, the buyer of the cargo, or some third party that solely arranges the transportation of the cargo.

Charterer

A person or organization that contracts to acquire a vessel for a voyage or a period of time to carry his cargo.

Freight Forwarder

An increasing importance is being placed upon the freight forwarder as he takes over many of the functions of the traditional shipowner/carrier yet remains interested in the cargo.

Many of the larger exporting companies maintain an in-house shipping and distribution department that negotiates contracts of affreightment or carriage of goods for the company with the shipping line that trades to the area of the world where the company's goods are destined.

However, there could probably be a lack of knowledge of exporting procedures and a lack of expertise for negotiating in a smaller company that exports.

Traditionally, the freight forwarder filled the need for expertise with their knowledge of export/import documentation and procedure, plus their wide experience in dealing with shipping companies with regard to contracts and documents.

The freight forwarder can offer services that come under four distinct headings

- Purely as a shipper's agent, procuring transport and shipping services on behalf of the exporter and under his direction
- As a forwarder offering a total expertise package to the exporter with regard to routing and choice of mode together with ancillary documentation and perhaps packing service. With regard to transport, he remains an agent for the exporter and bills of lading are made out in the shipper's name and to the shipper's account
- As a principal, usually multimodal transport operator, taking responsibility for the goods irrespective of who actually carries them. In many cases, he may be the actual carrier for at least part of the transit. He issues the transport documents, combined bill of lading.
- As a specialist provider of ancillary self-standing services, such as custom clearance, warehousing, packing, and port agency

Ancillary Services

- Brokers
- Insurers
- Surveyors
- Classification societies
- Flag state officials
- Port management

- Stevedores
- Port authorities
- Coast guard

Broker

The first of these headings is of relevance because of the countless persons I meet who calls himself a "broker."

In relation to shipping, the term *broker* covers a wide and varied list of activities

> Agents employed (at a customary or agreed rate of commission or remuneration) to buy or sell goods, merchandise or marketable securities, or to negotiate insurance, freight rates or other matters, for a principal; the sales or transaction being negotiated not in his own name but in the name of the principal. (*Marine Encyclopaedic Dictionary*)

More specifically brokers connected with the maritime industry can be categorized as follows:

Insurance brokers, who act as the intermediary between the ship-/cargo owner and the underwriters when marine insurance is negotiated. This form of broker could be an individual, but more likely, it will be part of a large organization providing a global service of insurance, consultancy, risk management, and information.

Shipbrokers, who can be further divided into the following:

- *Sale and purchase brokers*, who buy and sell ships for clients (principals) or arrange contracts for building new ships
- *Shipowner's brokers*, who act for the shipowner with a ship to charter for a voyage; he is approached by the shipowner with a view of finding cargo to carry.
- *Loading broker/liner brokers*, who represent the shipowner or shipping line at the port of loading. He advertises the date of

sailing in shipping publications, obtains cargo, and coordinates the arrangements for delivery to the ship and loading, though the actual stowage is decided upon by the cargo superintendent and the ship's officers. It can also be this broker's business to sign the bill of lading on behalf of the master and issue it to the shipper (cargo owner) or his agent in exchange for freight, if freight is to be paid in advance.
- *Charterer's or merchant's broker*, who acts for the cargo interest and finds ships for the cargo; they will tend to specialize in a particular area or commodity.
- *Chartering brokers*, who act as intermediaries between the shipowner and the charterers or shippers and receivers. They are mostly responsible for the drafting or signing of the charter party.

The parties to the contract may use separate brokers or complete the fixture through the intervention of a mutual broker. This broker usually retains the original documents and issues certified copies to each party.

The broker's commission, paid by the shipowner, is generally specified in the charter party in the form of a stated percentage of the freight (voyage) or hire (time).

- *Forwarding agent* is employed by the shipper to find a ship, usually on a liner trade, to carry his cargo. It is the forwarding agent's normal duty to ascertain the date and place of sailing, obtain a space allocation, and prepare the bill of lading.

As different shipping lines tend to have their own form of bill of lading, it is the duty of the forwarding agent to obtain the correct bill of lading, complete it with the necessary particulars, and forward it to the loading broker for signing.

His other duties often include arranging for the goods to be brought alongside the ship, making custom entries and paying any dues on the cargo.
After shipment, the forwarding agent collects the completed (signed) bill of lading and sends it to the shipper.

The forwarding agent will also be employed by the consignee to collect the delivered goods and arrange the inward customs clearance and formalities.

Ship's agent/shipping agent, though technically not a broker, the ship's agent does attend to the shipowner's commercial needs and formalities before, during, and after the ship's stay in port.

The ship's agent represents the shipowner with regard to the official requirements needed for the ship to enter port, arranging with the port authorities for the allocation of berthing space to load/unload the ship, advising import and export cargo owners, or the forwarding agent and loading/unloading the cargo.

The ship's agent will also attend to the customs requirements of the port and pay (to be later reimbursed by the shipowner) all charges and dues the ship incurs.

The agent can often be nominated by the charterer and paid for by the owner. In this case, he could have a conflict of interest, where he is nominally acting for the ship but primarily puts the charterer's interest first. Care must be taken in approaching charterer's named agents, and ships should be advised to contact the ship manager's office on a secure line for advice.

If the shipping company is little used or even unknown to the ship's agent company, they will usually be ask for advance sums of money to pay disbursements and cash advances to the crew.

Apart from the commercial duties, the ship's agent will also look after the ship's noncommercial activities, crew replacement, repatriation and arranging stores, bunkers, water, and money.

With passenger ships, the agent handles all that is needed for the embarkation and disembarkation of the passengers.
Chartering agents are brokers who undertake the import and/or export of commodities in large quantities; they act as an intermediary between the owner and consignee of the goods.

Brokers thus appear to discharge well-developed and separate functions, but in practice, the activities of firms may include more than one of these functions, and the same firm is often acting for both parties, e.g., loading broker and forwarding agent.

Surveyors

Surveyors is a general term used by anybody wanting to inspect the ship or its cargo, its procedures or operation.

They can be associated with the following:

- The company superintendents, auditors, etc.
- Quality/SEP/ISM code
- P & I clubs
- Underwriters
- Classification societies
- Flag state authorities
- Port state authorities
- Cargo
- Possible buyer of vessel

Independent Surveyor

There is no such person as an *independent surveyor*—all surveyors are contracted to work for some person or organization, and they must be dealt with in a careful manner.

In many cases, the office will request the ship for permission for a surveyor's visit and will provided his details, such as name and organization.

On all occasions, identification must be requested and, when in doubt, refuse permission to board until the office has been contacted.
Time must be spent showing them the ship and its operation though company confidentiality must be respected. In areas of doubt, ship's masters are advised to contact the management office and *ask*.

Time must be spent showing them the ship and its operation.

To proceed on its voyage, a vessel must use the necessary brokers and agents.

Classification Societies

Ship classification societies set and maintain standards of safety and reliability.

They provided this service to the shipper and insurer before the days of statutory control on the way ships were to be constructed and the equipment they were to carry.

Because of this, a trust was established between the classification society and the shipping industry, and if a ship was "in class" or was given a the class A1 Lloyd's, the cargo owner or underwriter could be confident that the ship was well found and had been built to the highest possible standard, that she had been surveyed during the building process and all her ancillary equipment, i.e., engines, plates, etc., had also been surveyed and passed as complete. Once the ship was classed by the society, it had to maintain an extensive and regular survey schedule to maintain that class; this would entail dry-docking under the society's supervision, onboard inspections, and dismantling of potentially hazardous equipment for detailed examination, e.g., boilers.

The shipowner could gain by having his ship in class be obtaining more favorable insurance rates and better chartering arrangements.

Present-day classification societies provide more than just classing and surveying ships; they also provide the following:

- Independent inspection agencies for states to use as supplementary to their own government surveyors
- Impartial exclusive surveyors who work in the interests of their principle with regard to building, accident, and buying surveys

- A comprehensive shipping information service (Lloyd's Register of Ships is probably the oldest (first printed 1764) and the best known.)
- A marine advisory service on most subjects connected with the technical aspects of ship operations
- Auditing of quality systems established by ship operators
- An extensive service in small boat building, heavy industry, nondestructive testing, safety technology, engineering advise, quality assurance, and the offshore industry

With the advent of international organizations, like the International Maritime Organization, the classification societies realized that their control was being superseded by state legislation over which they usually had little control; therefore in 1968, they formed an international association to protect their interests and to provide a unified voice in promoting improvements that they felt vital to the expanding technically complex shipping industry.

International Association of Classification Societies (IACS). The main aim of IACS was to maintain close cooperation with the world's maritime industries and to consult and cooperate with relevant international and maritime organizations in the promotion of improvements of standards of safety at sea.

The topics covered by IACS include the following:

- Bulk chemicals
- Containers
- Drilling units
- Electrical
- Engines
- Fire protection
- Gas tankers Gas tankers
- Inland waterway ships
- Marine pollution
- Materials and welding
- Mooring and anchoring
- Pipes and pressure ships
- Strength of ships
- Subdivisions, stability, and load lines
- Survey reporting and certification

Classification societies provide a useful and necessary service; there are often doubts expressed about their impartiality and their commercialism, but overall, the shipping industry must be a safer place with the knowledge that most of them provide a worthwhile and noteworthy system of accreditation.

2. International Regulations

When the shipping company has decided how to obtain the ship it needs, its next decision will be one on the flag or nationality of the ship.

The traditional view of ships "belonging" to the country where the owner has his business has long been out of favor.

The contemporary attitude of shipowners regarding the flag of the ship is no longer based on the plaintive cries of reactionary maritime nation's

- ♦ National economies
- ♦ Defense
- ♦ Pride of flag

But on simple economics and the realities of a commercial enterprise.

If a United States ship can be operated for a third of the cost under the Liberian flag, the US shipping company will need a very strong commercial inducement to register under the US administration rather than the Liberian.

Flag

The flag of the vessel is the state where the vessel is registered.

In most cases, the difference in attitudes regarding registration requirements can be associated with the traditions a country has with the shipping industry.

Some countries with a tradition of maritime activities have very strict requirements for approving vessel registration:

- *United States.* Shipowner needs to be a US citizen or US registered company. The vessel requires to have been built in the USA. The crew needs to be (on the whole) US citizens.
- *reece.* Shipowner needs to be Greek or of a Greek company. Crew needs to be Greek citizens, though some allowance are made, but pay must comply with strict marine laws regarding pay and conditions.

Other traditional maritime states have a more pragmatic view on registration:

- *United Kingdom.* Shipowner needs to have a percentage of UK ownership.
- *Germany* allows dual registration.
- *Norway* invented a "new" domain to allow owners to put their vessels under Norwegian law for some items but not others (e.g., crew conditions).

Open Registers

Many non-traditional maritime countries, however, have applied an open register system that allows any foreign person, company, or organization to register a vessel under its laws. They have no restrictions on the nationality of owner or crew, they do not impose financial burdens by way of tax, and they have a limited infrastructure for the management of their vessels, relying mainly on private organizations and classification societies to control their flagged vessels' technical operation. These countries are often referred to as *flags of convenience.*

Registration

Registration provides a ship with a national identity and should give the ship and crew some degree of protection when dealing with other states.

It provides jurisdiction for incidents occurring on board the ship when the ship is on the high seas.

It further provides other states with a recognized procedure for dealing with events that occur in their coastal waters or on the high seas.

Under various conventions, UNCLOS III, UNCTAD, United Nations Convention on Conditions for the Registration of Ships (1986), ILO (107 of 1958) and IMO resolutions (A.441 (XI)), an attempt has been made by international legislators to have a genuine link with state of registration and the ship's owner.

The assembly invites every state to take necessary steps to ensure that the owner of a ship that flies its flag provides such state with current information to enable it to identify and contact the person responsible for that ship with regard to matters relating to maritime safety (IMO resolution A.441 (XI)).

Thus the registration of the ship provides a statutory system under which the ship should be operated both nationally and internationally.

However, the commercial life of the ship is little affected by the flag that it flies; apart from certain states' protectionism and the muted rumblings of the 40/40/20 convention on liner conferences, most cargo owners are more concerned about freight rates and service levels than they are about registration.

Where pressure can be applied is through the ITF and their practice of stopping ships from operating in a port when it has a crew that is considered to be underpaid. To overcome this problem, some charterers demand that the ship has a blue ticket from the ITF that gives some immunity from delays based on crew's wages.

Similarly, the flag of a ship has little influence with regard to insurance and classification societies, where the value of the owner weighs heavier than the nationality of the ship, especially where many of the less traditional flag states use the classification societies to issue their statutory certificates.

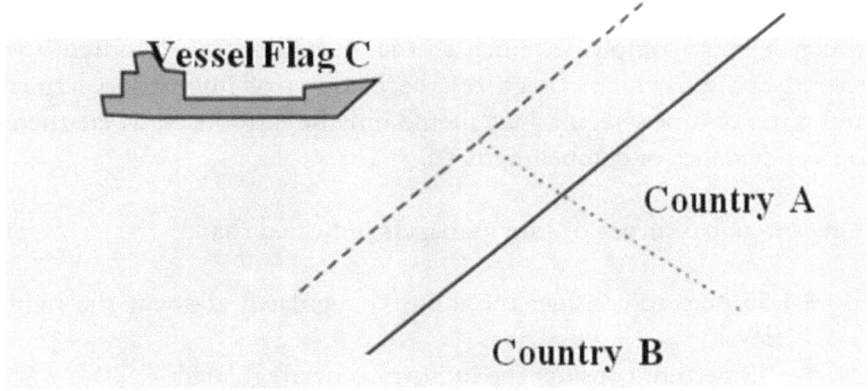

Jurisdiction

The vessel is registered with a country register. While the vessel is on the high seas, it is solely governed by the laws, rules, and regulations of that country. Safety and pollution law, pay and conditions of the crew, and all other legal aspects are controlled by the flag state.

Once the vessel enters the waters of a particular state, e.g., country B, it *must* comply with that state's laws; this is known as *port state control*.

It is normal for a port state not to interfere with the social aspects of shipboard life, but they will certainly become involved in safety, pollution, and operational aspects.

Flag State

Under the customary role of the law of the sea, it is the flag state that dictates the law relating to the ship.

It is on this premise that the IMO acts, laws, and regulations are passed and implemented.

Since its inception in 1958, the International Maritime Organization has adopted and amended existing conventions and instigated others, such that the shipping industry has countless items of legislation with which it must comply, so much so that resolution five hundred was recently passed which recognizes the plethora of international rules and states that new regulations should only be introduced where there is clear evidence of compelling need.

A recent global survey of ship managers indicated that

- 55 percent consider the industry regulated at about the right level
- 32 percent consider the industry is overregulated
- 13 percent consider the industry is underregulated

Maritime Legislation

Legislation now exists that covers most aspects of the ship and its commercial activities, and these regulations can be grouped into four areas:

- Ship
- Crew
- Environment
- Safety management
- Others

These categories are not and can never be thought of as separate; they overlap, and certain conventions apply to them individually while others apply to them all.

Ship

International legislation regarding the ship and the safety of the ship consists of the following:

- Safety of Life at Sea Convention (SOLAS) (1974)
- Convention on Load Lines (1966)
- Convention on Tonnage Measurement of Ships (1969)

SOLAS

SOLAS consists of nine chapters covering all aspects of shipboard safety; it extends the legislation to all seagoing ships (except fishing boats, which are legislated for by the Torremolinos convention (1979)).

SOLAS covers
- Certification that all ships require showing that they comply with the regulations with regard to
  - cargo ship safety construction
  - cargo ship safety equipment
  - cargo ship safety radio
  - passenger ship safety certificate
  - exemption certificate (chapter i)
- Construction, with regard to subdivision and stability, machinery and electrical installations, fire protection, fire detection and fire extinction (chapter 2)
- Lifesaving appliances and arrangements (chapter 3)
- Radio communications (chapter 4)
- Safety of navigation (chapter 5)
- Carriage of cargoes (chapter 6)
- Carriage of dangerous goods, which implement the International Gas Carrier (IGC) Code and the International Bulk Chemical (IBC) Code (chapter 7)
- Nuclear ships (chapter 8)
- Management for the safe operation of ships (chapter 9)
- Safety measures for high-speed craft (chapter 10)
- Special measures to enhance maritime safety (chapter 11)

Load Line

The limitations on the draft to which a ship may load are a significant factor in the safety of that ship. IMO recognizes this fact and are sponsors of this 1966 convention.

The legislation has regulations relating to the following:

- Watertight integrity of the ship's hull
- Additional safety with regard to doors and openings in the weather deck and hull
- Providing stability information for ships
- Marking the ship with her load line

Tonnage

The aim of the parties to the convention was to establish uniform principles and rules to determine the tonnage of ships engaged on international voyages.

The regulations define two tonnages:

- Gross tonnage—the total under deck volume of the ship
- Net tonnage—the cargo carrying volume of the ship

Crew

Most legislation pertaining to the crew's welfare and conditions is adopted through the International Labour Organization, though IMO have produced some legislation on crew, from a safety point of view.

- Age limits (ILO 58/1936)
- Medical certificate (ILO 73/1946)
- Minimum standards (ILO 147/1976)
- Standards of training, certification, and watchkeeping (STCW) (IMO 1978)

Minimum Standards (ILO 147)

The convention was adopted as one way of dealing with substandard ships, especially those registered under flags of convenience.

It applies to every seagoing ship engaged in the transport of cargo or passengers.

Article 2 of the convention lays down the areas that the minimum standards are to be applied:

- Safety standards, hours of work, and manning
- Social security measures
- Shipboard conditions of employment and living arrangements
- Engagement of crew and complaints procedure
- Properly qualified and trained seafarers
- Official inquiries into serious marine casualties

A state that has ratified the convention may take all measures necessary to rectify any conditions on board a ship of a different flag that enters its port in the normal course of business that does not conform to the standards set by the convention and which are clearly hazardous to safety and health (article 4.1).

This is a divergence from the long-accepted view that the flag state controls the standards of the ship and the emergence of the principle of port state control.

STCW Convention

Early on in the development of the IMO, attention was drawn to the need to have suitably educated and trained seafarers manning ships; the training should be in the use of the following:

- Aids to navigation
- Lifesaving equipment
- Fire prevention and extinction equipment
- Other ship's equipment contributing to safety

STCW provides the basis on which states can establish a common standard regarding certification and watchkeeping.

It lays down the following:

- The minimum standards and numbers for the various classes of engine, radio, and deck officer certificates required
- The special requirements for tankers, gas, and chemical carriers regarding the training of the master, officers, and ratings
- The standards of proficiency required in survival craft

Individual states that ratify this convention must implement its regulations into their national legislation such that it will apply on ships that sail under their flag.

However, one important feature of STCW is that it applies to ships of nonparty states when they are visiting ports of states that are parties to the convention, and these visiting ships are to be given no more favorable treatment than a ship that belongs to a state that has accepted the convention (article X).

Once again, the doctrine of flag state jurisdiction and control is breached, and port states are encouraged to enforce regulations on nonconvention flag ships.

STCW 78 was extensively amended in July 1995; the revised version of the convention is known as STCW 95.

STCW 95 entered into force in its revised form on February 1, 1997. It incorporates an STCW code to which many technical regulations have been transferred. Generally speaking, the revised convention contains basic requirements that are enlarged and explained in the code. Part A of the code is mandatory (and contain, for example, tables of minimum standards required of seafarers) while part B is recommended and contains guidance intended to help with the implementation of the convention. Regulations are divided in this way to make future amendments easier to introduce; there is no need to call a full conference to update a code.

Under chapter 1, reg.7, parties are required to provide detailed information to IMO concerning administrative procedures taken to ensure compliance with the convention, education and training courses, certification procedures and other factors relevant to implementation. This information will be used by IMO's maritime safety committee to identify complying parties. Other parties will then be able to accept certificates issued by these parties. No proof of compliance was required under the original convention.

Until February 1, 2002, parties may continue to issue, recognize, and endorse certificates that applied before this date in respect of seafarers who began training or seagoing service before August 1, 1998.

Other important amendments to chapter 1 (general provisions) include the following:

- Enhanced procedures concerning exercise of port state control;
- Parties are required to establish procedures for investigating acts by persons to whom they have issued certificates that endanger safety or the environment;
- Technical innovations, such as different working practices and the use of simulators for training purposes, have been recognized. Simulators will become mandatory for training in the use of radar and ARPA. Parties are required to ensure that training, certification and other procedures are continuously monitored by means of a quality-assurance system;
- Medical standards are contained in reg. 9. Certificates must be issued showing that levels of fitness have been met, particularly regarding eyesight and hearing;
- Every master, officer, and radio operator is required at intervals of not more than five years to meet the fitness standards prescribed in reg. 9 and the level of professional competence contained in section A-i/11 of the STCW code;
- A reference is made in reg. 14 to the ISM code. The regulation details further company responsibilities for manning, certification, record keeping, shipboard familiarization, and crew coordination.

The remaining chapters contain regulations concerning specific departments and ranks. Chapter 2, for example, deals with the master and deck department, and chapter 3 with the engine department.

Special requirements have been introduced in chapter 5 concerning training and qualifications of personnel on certain types of ship.

Emergency, occupational safety, medical care, and survival functions have been introduced in chapter 6.

Regulations concerning the functional approach to training are introduced in chapter 7.

Requirements concerning minimum rest period are introduced in chapter 8.

Crew Agreements

Contracts of employment between the shipowner/manager and the crew of the ship have always been a cause of much contention.

Theoretically, the flag state controls, through national legislation, the welfare and conditions of its ship's seamen, and a shipping company has little room for maneuver regarding such items that concern its employees as follows:

- Accommodation
- Feeding
- Repatriation
- Treatment for sickness

While not covered by legislation, crew's pay and leave conditions are normally negotiated for by unions and seamen's organizations, allowing the shipowner slightly more flexibility in gaining the maximum benefit that he can.

In reality though, the shipowner of a nontraditional shipping state can, and often does, employ seafarers from third-party states with little regard for the niceties of national or international law.

The problems encountered in some parts of the world makes the blue certificate accreditation of the ITF important.

Indeed, charterers often insist on it being applied for and carried on board the ship to reduce the possibilities of delays and detention.

Shipboard agreements must be carried and displayed, and any discrepancies between the ship agreement and the seaman's shore contract should be identified at the time of signing on, or engagement, and steps should be taken immediately to rectify a possible area of contention and problem.

Environment

Protection of the environment is an important issue, and the shipping industry can go a long way to improve the standards of its anti-pollution measures.

One of the most effective means of combating marine pollution is by educating and training the operating personnel

- Employed on board ships
- Involved in the management of ships
- Administering the export/import port

To assist in this education, there are many pieces of legislation relating to pollution prevention:

- UNCLOS III (UN Conference on the Law of the Sea III)
- International Convention for the Prevention of Pollution from Ships (MARPOL 1973 and protocols)
- Convention for the Prevention of the Pollution of the Sea by Oil (OILPOL 1954 and amendments)
- Convention on the Prevention of Marine Pollution by Dumping of Wastes and Other Matter 1972
- SOLAS 1974, chapter 7

MARPOL is the most important single document concerned with preventing marine pollution; it covers five categories of pollutants:

- Oil
- Noxious liquid substances in bulk
- Harmful substances in package form
- Sewage
- Garbage

The annexes concerning oil (annex 1), noxious liquid substances (annex 2), harmful substances (annex 3), and garbage (annex 5) are all in force.

MARPOL includes provisions on reducing/preventing pollution by

- Operational methods, e.g., Dilution rates for oil and noxious liquids, crude oil washing
- Constructional methods, e.g., Wing tanks, segregated ballast, loading areas
- Shoreside methods, reception facilities

Important aspects of the MARPOL regulations also include the provision for a Shipboard Oil Pollution Emergency Plan (SOPEP).

This document is prepared by the ship operator, and after accreditation by the flag state or a classification society acting for it, a copy is carried on board the ship and acts as a contingency plan for actual and possible oil pollution incidents.

Other

The international agencies associated with the United Nations have produced many conventions, some obviously more relevant to shipping operations than others. This final section covers the legislation that is not easy to categorize under ship, crew, and environment, though, of course, it is associated with all three.

- Convention on the International Regulations for the Prevention of Collision at Sea (COLREGS) 1972
- Convention on Maritime Search and Rescue (MERSAR) 1979
- International Convention for Safe Containers 1972
- International Maritime Dangerous Goods Code (IMDG)
- International Safety Management (ISM) Code

COLREGS 1972

The "rules of the road," associated with the safe passage and navigation of a ship through traffic.

The regulations that determine which ship has the right-of-way in a possible two-ship, non-reduced-visibility collision situation. Both have the responsibility to avoid a collision, but one has the initial responsibility to take action first while the other is the "stand on ship."

In reduced visibility, both must take action, a maneuver that will not jeopardize the action of the other.

Under the COLREGS, ship must display certain lights—port, red; starboard, green; masthead lights, white; etc.—and shapes—a ball for an anchored ship, a cylinder for a ship constrained by its draft, and "two black balls in a vertical line" for a ship not under command.

One of the most important aspects of the COLREGS is the implementation of the traffic separation schemes that keep ships to recognized routes at concentration points around the land.

International Safety Management (ISM) Code

Introduction

Accidents over the last few years involving passenger ships and ships carrying harmful substances have highlighted the need for good operational standards and onboard procedures. These standards and procedures are primarily the concern of the flag state, but in many instances, port states have taken a proactive role in ensuring vessels comply with at least the minimum standards set out in SOLAS, MARPOL, and STCW.

The IMO have recognized that ships need good management and control and have set out an appropriate system for the organization of management of ships through the International Management Code for the Safe Operation of Ships and for Pollution Prevention—International Safety Management (ISM) Code (IMO resolution A741 (18)—1993).

A copy of the document of compliance and the safety management certificate must be carried onboard the vessel.

Objectives (1.2)

The objectives of the code are to ensure safety at sea, prevention of human injury or loss of life, and avoidance of damage to the environment, in particular to the marine environment, and to property.

Each company must have safety management objectives to

- Provide for safe practices in ship operation and a safe working environment
- Establish safeguards against all identified risks
- Continuously improve safety management skills of personnel ashore and aboard ships, including preparing for emergencies related to safety and environmental protection.

Implementation

By June 1, 1998, signatory governments to the ISM code should have implemented its use for all passenger ships, oil tankers, chemical tankers, gas carriers, bulk carriers, and cargo high-speed craft of five hundred gross tonnage and upward. Other cargo vessels and mobile offshore drilling units of five hundred gross tonnage and upward must be covered not later than July 1, 2002.

Document of Compliance (13.2)

When a company that owns or manages vessels complies with the requirements of the ISM code, it will be issued with a document of compliance. The document will be issued

- ♦ By the administration of the vessel owned or operated,
- ♦ By an organization recognized by the administration, or
- ♦ By the government, on behalf of the administration, of the country in which the company operates.

The document will be displayed in the management office and must be also carried on board the vessel. The document should be accepted as evidence that the company is capable of complying with the requirements of the ISM code.

The renewal survey/audits are at five-year intervals, with annual intermediate survey/audits.

Safety Management Certificate (13.4)

A certificate called a safety management certificate (SMC) should be issued to a ship by the administration or a recognized authority verifying that its managing company and its shipboard management operate in accordance with the approved safety management system.

The SMC should be issued to a ship following an initial verification of compliance with the requirements of the ISM. This includes the verification that DOC for the company responsible for the operation of the ship is applicable to that particular type of ship and assessment of the shipboard SMS to verify that it complies with the requirements of the ISM code and that it is implemented. Objective evidence demonstrating that the company's SMS has been functioning effectively for at least three months on board the ship should be available, including, inter alia, records from the internal audit performed by the company.

The SMC is valid for a period of five years.

The validity of the SMC is subject to at least one intermediate verification, confirming the effective functioning of the SMS and that any modifications carried out since the previous verification comply with the requirements of the ISM code. In certain cases, particularly during the initial period of operation under the SMS, the administration may find it necessary to increase the frequency of the intermediate verification. Additionally, the nature of nonconformities may also provide a basis for increasing the frequency of intermediate verifications.

Only the issuing administration may withdraw the SMC. The issuing administration should withdraw the SMC if intermediate verification is not requested or if there is evidence of major nonconformity with the ISM code.

Interim DOC and SMC

In cases of change of flag or company, special transitional arrangements should be made.

An interim DOC, valid for no more than twelve months, may be issued to facilitate initial implementation of the ISM code and implementation where a company is newly established or where new ship types are added to an existing DOC.

An interim SMC, valid for not more than six months, may be issued to new ships on delivery and when a company takes on the responsibility for the management of a ship which is new to the company. In special cases, the administration may extend the validity of the interim SMC for a further six months.

Safety Management System (SMS) (1.4)

To comply with the code every company must develop, implement and maintain a safety management system (SMS) which will include the following:

- ♦ A safety and environmental protection policy

- Defined levels of authority and lines of communication between and among shore and shipboard personnel
- Instructions and procedures to ensure safe operation of ships and protection of the environment in compliance with relevant international and flag state legislation
- Procedures for reporting accidents and nonconformities (breaches) with the provisions of the code
- Procedures to prepare for and respond to emergency situations
- Procedures for internal audits of the system and management reviews

Safety Management Policy (2.1)

The company must establish a policy that describes how the safety management objectives of the company will be achieved.

Development of Plans for Shipboard Operations (7)

The company should establish procedures for preparing plans and instructions for key shipboard operations concerning the safety of the ship and the prevention of pollution.

Company Responsibilities and Authority (3)

The company should define and document the responsibility, authority, and interrelation of all personnel who manage, perform, and verify work relating to and affecting safety and pollution prevention.

Emergency Preparedness (8)

The company should establish procedures to identify, describe, and respond to potential emergency shipboard situations. These procedures should be tested in drills and exercises.

The safety management system should provide for measures ensuring the company's organization can respond at any time to hazards, accidents, and emergencies involving its managed ships.

Reports and Analysis (9)

The safety management system should include procedures ensuring that non-conformities, accidents and hazardous situations are reported to the company, investigated and analyzed with the objective of improving safety and pollution prevention.

Human Resources

Designated Person (4)

To ensure the safe operation of each ship and to provide a link between the company and those on board, each company should designate a person ashore having direct access to the highest level of management. The responsibility and authority of the designated person should include monitoring the safety and pollution prevention aspects of the operation of each ship and to ensure that adequate resources and shore-based support are applied as required.

Master's Responsibility and Authority (5)

The company should clearly outline and document the master's responsibility regarding:

- Implementing the safety and environmental protection policy of the company
- Motivating the crew in complying with of the policy
- Issuing appropriate orders and instructions in a clear and simple manner
- Verifying that specified requirements are observed
- Reviewing the safety management system and reporting its deficiencies to shore-based management

The company should ensure that the safety management system operating on board the ship contains a clear statement emphasizing the master's authority.

Qualifications and Training (6)

The company should ensure that the master is

- Properly qualified for command
- Fully conversant with the company's safety management system
- Given the necessary support so that the master's duties can be safely performed

The company should ensure that each vessel is manned with relevant qualified and certificated and medically fit seafarers. These seafarers should be given proper familiarization with their duties. Information or instruction, which is essential and should be provided prior to sailing, must be identified, documented, and issued.

The company should ensure that all personnel involved in the safety management system have an adequate understanding of relevant rules, regulations, codes, and guidelines.
Training is essential for the proper compliance of the safety management system, and the company must establish and maintain procedures to ensure all personnel concerned receive relevant instruction.

All relevant information on the safety management system should be provided in the working language of the vessel.

Structure of a Safety Management System

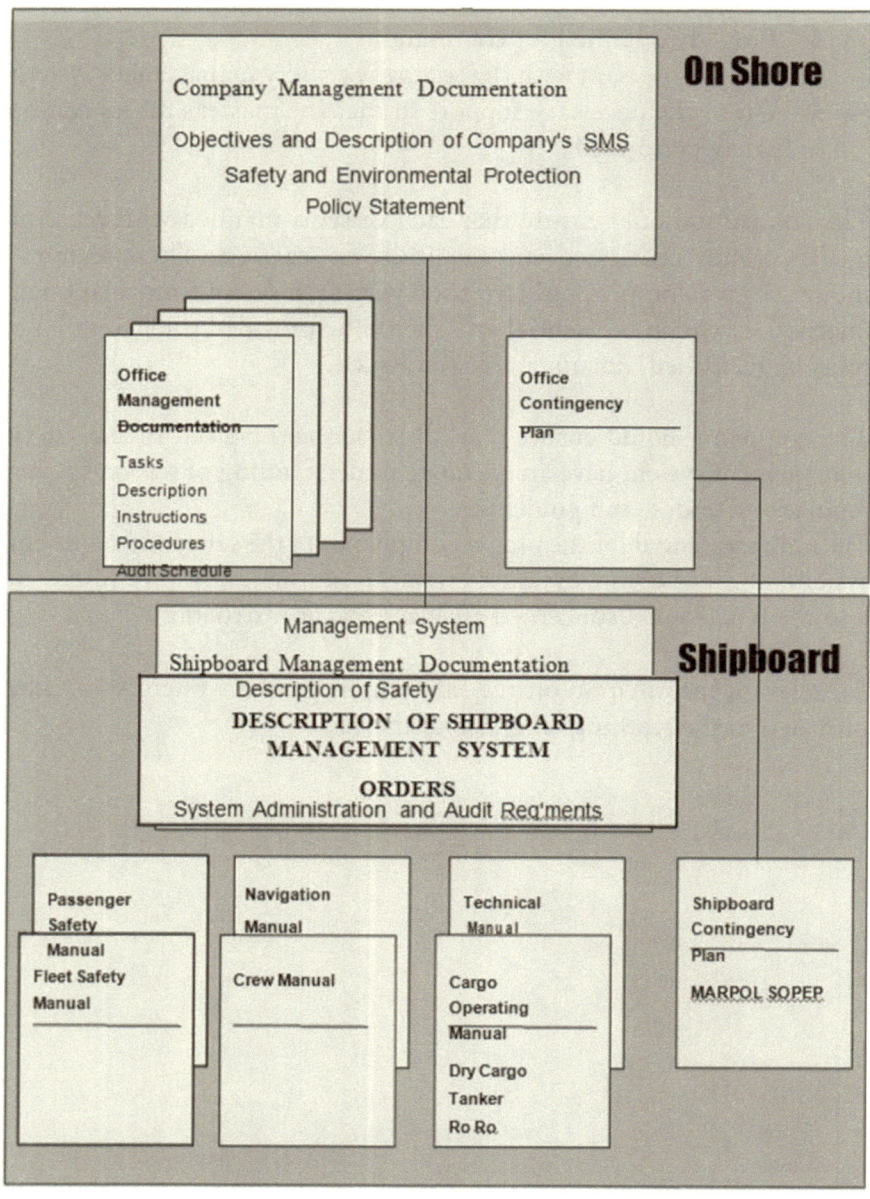

Maintenance of the Ship and Equipment (10)

Procedures must be established to ensure that the ship is technically maintained in conformity with the provisions of the relevant international and class rules and regulations.

In meeting these provisions, the company must ensure that

- Inspections are held at appropriate intervals
- Any nonconformity is reported with the possible cause
- Appropriate corrective action is taken
- Records are maintained

Equipment and technical systems whose failure could result in a hazardous situation must be identified, and specific measures should be recorded to promote the reliability of this equipment or system.

Documentation (11)

All documents and data which are relevant to the safety management system should be controlled, and the company should ensure that

- Valid documents are available at all relevant locations
- Changes to documents are reviewed and approved by authorized personnel
- Obsolete documents are promptly removed

Company Verification, Review, and Evaluation (12)

Internal audits must be carried out to establish that safety and pollution prevention activities comply with safety management system. In addition, the company should periodically review and evaluate the efficiency of the safety management system.

Personnel carrying out audits should be independent of the areas being audited.

The results of the audits should be brought to the attention of all relevant personnel, and management responsible for the audited area should take timely corrective action on deficiencies found.

Certification (13)

A copy of the document of compliance and a safety management certificate must be carried on board the vessel and be available for inspection by flag and port officials.

Conclusion

The ISM code sets out a strict regime for the operation of vessels. The management system implemented by the shipowner or manager must be well documented and be able to show that it is practical and usable. It must include information related to the following:

- Procedures to ensure the safe operation of ships and protection of the environment
- Procedures for key shipboard operations
- Procedures to ensure that the ship is maintained
- Procedures to identify, describe, and respond to potential emergency shipboard situations
- Levels of authority and lines of communication

The procedures should be tested in practice or by drills and exercises, and the company must have a procedure to ensure that nonconformities are reported to ensure that the system is used.

Without the implementation of a safety management system, vessels will not be allowed to trade.

As this is the case, shipowners and managers must soon identify which management system they will adopt for their organizations. Whether the shipping company is large or small, they must implement a system that is seen to be a quality system that complies with the International Safety Management Code.

Port State Control

During the late 1960s and 1970s, there was an increase in nontraditional maritime countries registering any vessel under their flag. This was seen by many coastal/port states as a reduction in the management and control by the flag state over their registered ships especially with regard to the prime responsibilities of safety and environmental protection.

From this and some particularly high profile oil spill incidents, certain states began a move toward port state control, where they could monitor and check vessels visiting their country. After initial survey and checks, it was possible to ban vessels from sailing or even bar them from entering the territorial waters of the country.

Four international port state control agreements are currently in force:

- Paris Memorandum of Understanding
- Latin American Agreement (Acuerdo de Vina del Mar)
- Tokyo Memorandum of Understanding (Asia-Pacific MOU), and
- Caribbean Memorandum of Understanding.

The Mediterranean MOU, signed in July 1987, is expected to be implemented two years from this date.

The Paris Memorandum of Understanding on port state control (MOU) was adopted in January 1982.

It is an agreement between fifteen West European states to enforce an effective system of port state control.

The port state control will ensure that, without discrimination as to flag, foreign merchant ships visiting its ports comply with the standards laid down in international conventions on the safety of ships, crews, and the environment (section 1.2), ships of member states are regarded as "foreign."

The conventions that are applicable to the MOU are as follows:

- Safety of Life at Sea (SOLAS)
- Load line
- Standards of Training, Certification, and Watchkeeping (STCW)
- Collision Regulations (COLREGS)
- Prevention of pollution from ships (MARPOL)
- Minimum standards (ILO no. 147, section 2.1)

To achieve the memorandum's aim of preventing the operation of substandard ships, states are required to inspect and survey the ships that visit their ports.

Each state will accomplish this by an annual total inspection corresponding to 25 percent of the estimated number of individual foreign merchant ships that entered the ports of the state during a recent respective period of twelve months (section 1.3).

In fulfilling their commitments, states will carry out inspections, which will consist of a visit on board a ship in order to check certificates and documents relevant for the purposes of the memorandum.

In the absence of valid certificates or documents or if there are clear grounds for believing that the ship does not substantially meet the requirements of a relevant convention, a more detailed inspection will be carried out (section 3.1).

The state will regard as "clear grounds" the following:

- A report from another member state
- A report or complaint by the master or crew or any organization with a legitimate interest in the safe operation of the ship, shipboard living and working conditions or the prevention of pollution, unless the state concerned deems the report as manifestly unfounded
- Other indications of serious deficiencies (section 3.2)

In selecting ships for inspection, the state will pay particular attention to

- Ships that may present a special hazard, for instance, oil tankers and gas and chemical carriers
- Ships that have had several recent deficiencies. States will seek to avoid inspecting ships that have been inspected by any other member state within the previous six (6) months, unless they have clear grounds for inspection (section 3.4).

To assist port states in this requirement, ships can request a letter of compliance from the surveyor showing date and place of inspection and that the ship complied with the requirements of the MOU.

Each state will endeavor to secure the rectification of deficiencies detected (section 3.6).

In the case of deficiencies that are clearly hazardous to safety, health, or the environment, the port state will ensure that the hazard is removed before the ship is allowed to proceed to sea to ensure this the ship can be detained (section 3.7).

Where deficiencies cannot be remedied in the port of inspection, the state may allow the ship to proceed to another port, subject to any appropriate conditions determined with a view to ensuring the ship can proceed without unreasonable danger to health, safety, or the environment; in such circumstances, the port state will notify the state where the next port of call of the ship is situated (section 3.8).

The port state will, after an inspection, issue to the master of the ship a document giving the results of the surveys (section 3.10).

Often a situation arises where the flag state has not ratified a particular convention and thus does not have the administration or procedure to survey the ship and issue the relevant certificate.

In this case a shipowner can apply for a certificate of compliance from a classification society, who will survey and examine the ship as if it were a national survey.

Once they are satisfied as to the acceptable condition of the ship, they will issue the certificate. For example, a flag state may not be a party to MARPOL; therefore the company may apply for a certificate of compliance as an alternative to the International Oil Pollution Prevention (IOPP) certificate.

Annex 1

When surveying, the surveyor is to exercise his professional judgment in determining whether to detain the ship until the deficiencies are corrected or to allow it to sail with certain deficiencies without unreasonable danger to safety, health, or the environment (1.1.2).

Ships that are entitled to fly the flag of a state that is not a party to a relevant convention shall receive a detailed inspection following the same guidelines that are provided for a ship of a state that is a party to the convention (1.1.3).

The area covered by the Paris memorandum can be divided into three major parts

- ♦ Safety of the ship
  This comes under the conventions of SOLAS 1974 (plus 1978 protocol), load line, and COLREGS (section 2).

- ♦ Protection of the environment
  The MARPOL convention of 1973 (plus protocol 1978) provides the standards for this area (section 2).

- ♦ Crew
  The legislation for this area is contained in numerous ILO conventions implemented by ILO convention no. 147, and by the STCW convention, the main items of concern are as follows:
  - manning (section 3.2)
  - certification (section 3.3)
  - minimum age (section 4.2)
  - medical examination (section 4.3)

- food and catering (section 4.4)
- crew accommodation (section 4.5)
- accident prevention and occupational health (section 4.6)

◆ Small ships under 500 gross tonnage (section 5)

Annex 2

In cases of deficiencies not fully rectified or only provisionally repaired, a message using the format of this annex should be sent to the next port of call of the ship.

Annex 3

After an inspection, the master of the ship is to be given a detailed report.

Annex 4

Information system to be used by a participating state to the Central Administration at Saint-Malo (CAAM).

USCG Port State Control Initiative

The USCG identified substandard ships as a probable cause of safety and pollution incidents in their territorial waters and set up a port state control program to eliminate the problem.

The program's goal is to identify and eliminate substandard foreign vessels from US waters and to encourage persons committed to trading to the United States to adopt management philosophies that ensure compliance with accepted standards (section 1).

The program carries this out by systematically targeting high-risk vessels for boarding and inspection.

The initiative is for a boarding regime to target substandard ships, and its goal is to identify and eliminate substandard foreign vessels from US waters and encourage those committed to trading with the United States to adopt management philosophies that ensure compliance with accepted standards.

The initiative increases the frequency of boardings on high-risk ships. The risks involve threats to life, property, and the environment.

The high-risk ships are identified from their own previous records in addition to the records affecting their owner (operator), classification society, and flag state.

The Coast Guard achieves this by identifying high-risk vessels by key elements such as substandard

- Vessels
- Owners/managers
- Classification societies
- Flag states

Substandard Ship

Ship is regarded as substandard if the hull, crew, machinery, or equipment such as lifesaving, firefighting, and pollution prevention are substantially below the standards required by US law or international convention.

Substandard applies to the following:

    A. absence of principal equipment
    B. gross noncompliance with equipment standards
    C. substantial deterioration

Targeted Owner

It includes the owner, operator, managing operator of any vessel that is subject to a US intervention carried out under the authority of an international convention.

The designation applies to every vessel associated with the targeted owner, not just the vessel subjected to the intervention.

To maximize the effectiveness of Coast Guard actions, the boarding teams conduct their examinations at sea and in port.

Targeted Classification Society

A targeted classification society is one that has not been recognized by the Coast Guard as demonstrating compliance with the guidelines of the IMO and that has an intervention ratio exceeding the USCG limits.

Targeted Flag States

These are identified on a comparison of the vessel intervention ratios of various flag states, the number of vessels under that flag, and the number of visits to the United States.

To eliminate substandard ship operations in US waters, no-US vessels entering ports will be targeted according to a priority and risk factor. Those vessels *suspected* of presenting an imminent threat to life, the port, and the environment will be targeted for boarding prior to entry into port.

Priority 1 Vessels

- Stateless vessels
- Vessels suspected of hazarding the port or environment as a result of a hazardous materials release or an ongoing discharge of oil
- Vessels operated by targeted owned or operator, vessels flying flag of targeted flag, vessel operating under targeted classification society
- Seventeen points or more

Priority 2 Vessels

- Vessels that do not have Tank Vessel Examination (TVE)

- Vessels with overdue outstanding requirements issued at previous examinations
- Vessels that lack a record of previous USCG examination
- Seven points or more

Priority 3 Vessels

- Vessels that do not have or are past due for an annual freight vessel examination or quarterly passenger vessel reexamination
- Vessels alleged to be substandard by a member of the crew, a professional or other association, a trade union or any other interested person
- Four to six points

Priority 4 Vessels

- Vessels possessing none of the critical criteria.
- Zero to three points

Targeting Criteria

Each priority also possesses a points system based on the targeting criteria of the following:

Owner		Flag		Class		History		V/I type	
Ship owned by targeted owner or operator	7	Ship flagged to targeted state	7	Not listed as a recognized class	5	Subject to violation report	1 per case	Bulk chemical tanker	1
Ship going to facility frequently receiving substandard ships	2	No available performance record on state	7	Intervention ratio above USCG limits	3	Subject to operational control or detention	1 per case	Oil tanker	1
						Involved in marine casualty or oil/hazardous incident in last 12 months	1 per case	Gas carrier	1
								Bulk freighter 10 years or more	1
								Passenger ship	1
						Ship not boarded within 6 months	1	Ship carrying low-value commodity	1

To maintain a good record with the USCG, it is important to report all defects and correspondence to the management office.

Action must be taken to clear all defects before entering US waters.

Prevention through People

Human error causes more than 80 percent of marine casualties. The USCG is developing a long-term strategy to refocus prevention efforts on casualties caused by human error.

Ship Finance

External finance for shipping started in the 1950s as world trade grew, recovering after World War II.

Previously, shipping finance was funded from the shipowner's own cash flow, but this proved no longer sufficient to keep pace with growth and rising ship costs.

There are two points to note in ship finance that really set it apart from traditional commercial finance and why the market has been limited to specialist departments of major international banks in the United States and United Kingdom and to a number of continental banks whose main business interests are shipping finance.

Point 1: If a shipowner goes bankrupt, the supply of shipping is unchanged.

Contrast this fact with a manufacturing industry.

If a "widget" maker goes out of business, the plant and equipment are scrapped and the staff become unemployed and seek work elsewhere. The buildings and land are taken into other use. Thus, an economic mechanism quickly regulates such industries.

Clearly shipping does not respond in this way. A lower-cost operator will take advantage and buy ships from the bankrupt company to trade elsewhere.

Point 2: The second area in which shipping differs from other industries is in the provision of finance.

Finance tends to be short-term against an asset that has a long-term technical life, which generally, with adequate maintenance, is at least twenty years. Typical ship finance is five to ten years. This can give the shipowner cash flow problems if freight rates slump, as happened in the early 1980s.

The chances are that if a company decides to build a new ship or intends to purchase a quality ship secondhand, then the cost will have to be financed externally.

In a capital intensive and cyclical business like shipping, it should come as no great surprise that financing terms can make or break any given transaction.

On a project basis, the lender will want to know that the shipowner can service the loan and repay the capital throughout the agreed term.

Servicing the loan means paying interest, which will probably be at a variable rate, London interbank offered rate (LIBOR), plus a fixed differential. So if interest rates rise during the loan, the interest payments will increase. Similarly, if interest rates should fall, interest payments will decrease.

It also means repaying capital.

As the value of the ship is most likely to fall through time, due to wear, tear, and obsolescence, ignoring, of course, market factors, a bank would not accept sale of the ship as a means of repaying all the original loan.

Capital repayments are therefore required, generally in equal amounts throughout the loan period. These payments have to be met from the income generated by trading the ship: from hire, if on a time charter; from freight, if the ship is voyage chartered.

It is no good being able to meet interest and capital needs and not being able to pay for adequate repair and maintenance and pay crew wages. The bank will look at cash flow on a year-by-year basis to ensure this is adequate to cover the shipowner's liabilities in all areas.

This is the bank's prime concern: the shipowner's ability to repay loan plus interest. What return on capital the shipowner achieves, what the project return yield is, is of no more than passing interest to the bank.

What is collateral? Basically it is the security offered by the shipowner to the value of the loan.

Depending on the value of mortgage advanced, the ship itself will be the collateral or primary security for the loan. (Note: a mortgage is a lien or conditional conveyance of the ship or other property as security for payment of money.)

The lender will impose conditions that the mortgagor (i.e., the shipowner) must meet.

Typical conditions cover items such as follows:

- Insurance
- Flag of registry
- Management

Whatever collateral is offered, it will have to be insured to cover the usual trading and other risks. For the ship, the bank may demand a H & M valued policy, typically at least 110–130 percent of the outstanding loan amount and cover for war risks. The policy will be assigned to the lender. It is usual for the lender to require insurance to cover hull and machinery, P & I, war risks, mortgagee's interest, and loss of hire.

The quality and competence of the technical management of the ship will be of interest to the bank. There are many ways in which the commercial and technical management of the ship can affect its value and trading prospects, and these are of interest to the bank.

For example, if a long-term contract to carry bulk grain were terminated and replaced by a charter for sulfur in bulk, then maintenance costs (steelwork corrosion) may rise substantially. If the ship required extensive abnormal repairs or repairs over a certain sum, then the bank may require to be informed because of the impact on cash flow.

Similarly, if for any reason, a change in classification society were to be made, the bank would want to be informed of this fact and the reason for such a change.

The bank is likely to look closely at the off-hire record of ships let under time charters.

Finally, but most importantly from the lender's point of view, we discuss control. The bank will want to be 100 percent sure that it can gain control of its security in the event of default and foreclosure.

The concerns of the ship mortgage bank and the shipowner are different.

The shipowner generally has to take a long-term view. His business is to make a profit in the long term by trading the ship in whatever markets are viewed as giving the best return.

This may be in the spot market, or by time chartering aiming to fix and lock-in near the peaks of market cycles.

The owner's aim is also to generate an income and hence a positive return on investment, usually a mix of equity and borrowings.

The ship mortgage bank frequently takes a shorter term view.

For example, a new building may have a technical life of twenty years or more. Typically the duration of a loan on a new building is ten years. Over this period, about half the ship's life, the bank has one concern only, that is, that the shipowner has sufficient cash flow to be able to repay the loan in quarterly or semiannual installments and make the agreed interest payments.

The bank makes its money from fees charged in setting up and administering the loan and from the interest rate spread, i.e., the difference between the rate at which it borrows money and the rate at which it lends money.

So the bank's concern is cash flow. The shipowner's concern is with cash flow too and to achieve an adequate return on (equity) investment.

Loan Security

With the exception of liner shipping, the typical shipowning group is composed of a series of companies. Usually each ship is owned by a separate company.

This is for reasons of limitation of liability; that is, where there is a multi-ship fleet in theory, action cannot be taken against one ship for debts or other legal responsibilities of another ship in the fleet.

Most of the companies in the group exist solely to own a ship and have little or no financial substance except for a small amount of cash.

Recourse (financial protection) is required by the bank not only because the shipowner is normally a single-purpose company with little substance other than the ship but also because of risks with respect to employment.

Security, therefore, takes the form of a mortgage on the ship, assignment of the ship's earnings and insurances, and the corporate guarantee of the parent company or the personal guarantee of the shareholders.

The typical type of commercial bank finance for secondhand purchases is project finance; that is, the employment of the ship is expected to be adequate to cover operating expenses and repay the debt.

The Future

For a regular and adequate stream of new funds to flow through the industry, the shipowners are dependent on the following: a stable world economy, the policies of oil, and other companies with respect to transportation and the structure of their own industry.

The world economy is beyond the shipowners' control, as are the oil companies. Thus the only way the industry can meet the challenge for new capital in the 1990s is by adapting itself.

It certainly has the capacity to adjust, but it may mean some important changes in the way it is structured. For example

- ◆ The need for new ships together with shipowners' limited resources calls for outside capital,
- ◆ Shipowners should be willing to open their capital to outside investors, at least to some extent; if not, new investors will come in;
- ◆ Shipowners may be able to retain their autonomy through a separation of the ownership function from the management function with the creation of partnerships or joint ventures.

These ventures will either be organized around the largest companies in the industry, which will use them as a means to expand their business while minimizing their financial exposure or around groups of investors who will hire technical and commercial managers.

Medium-term charter agreements with end-users may reappear and form the basis of these new ventures. The financing will take the form of debt, equity, or leasing.

The end result may mean a consolidating or restructuring of the industry taking place over the next ten to fifteen years to achieve fleet replacement: this is the real challenge.

Exercise 1: Ship Finance

A shipowner is looking at two financial options to buy a vessel of $20 million.

Option 1:   60 percent loan over five years at a rate of interest of 10 percent

Option 2:   50 percent loan over ten years at a rate of interest of 5 percent

Explain which option would give a better trading position.

Cargo Operations

The importance of cargo to the shipping industry cannot be overstated; without goods to transport, there would be no need for ships.

Most ships are associated with the movement of cargo, whether it is containers from New York to Rotterdam, oil from the Gulf to Japan or iron ore from Vitoria to Hunterston, even passengers can be considered a two-legged cargo!

No tugboats would be needed if ships did not berth nor oceanographic survey ships would be needed to chart the seas if there were no ships sailing on them.

Probably the only area that would be unaffected by the movement of cargo would be the armed naval services of the world.

The commercial aspects of cargo operations can be categorized under the following headings:

- Types of maritime trade
- Contracts of affreightment

Types of Maritime Trade

Shipping operations can be divided into three broad categories

- Cargo
- Passenger
- Other

Cargo

This class of operation makes up about 90 percent of all ships plying the oceans. The commodities carried during cargo operations are as diverse as the types of ships that carry them. Each type of commodity and type of ship has its own peculiarities and special needs of operation.

Voyage Diagram

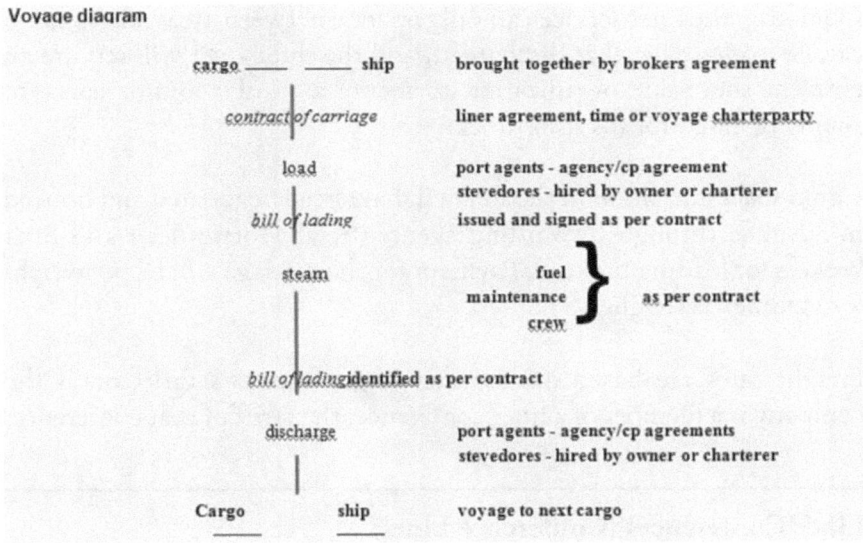

The main areas of cargo carrying operations are as follows

- Oil tankers
- Bulk carriers
- General cargo ships
- Container ships
- Gas and chemical carriers

Within these areas, the types of trade fall into two distinct divisions:

- Liner service   Tramp operations

Liner Service

On a liner service, the ship operates to a schedule; it trades on a specific route between advertised load and discharge ports on a regular basis.

The itinerary of the voyage will have been known for some time in the past, and its future will be known well in advance. This allows the shipowner to plan his ship's maintenance program and crew relief rotation.

Obviously the liner service can only operate between areas where cargo can be loaded as well as discharged, and the shipowner will require an efficient shore-side organization to secure a regular and/or constant supply of cargo for his ships to carry.

Cargo space allocation in the ship will have been negotiated and booked in advance through forwarding agents (freight forwarders) and liner brokers (or loading brokers). Payment for the carriage will be per weight (or volume) as freight.

Freight rates are based on the shipping company's tariff or, if the company is a member of a liner conference, the tariff of that conference.

Liner Conferences (Conference Lines)

An association of shipping companies of various nationalities running a liner service between the same general areas, e.g. Northwest Europe/west coast of South America.

The association (conference) will agree, among other things,

- ♦ To charge similar freight rates
- ♦ To limit the number of sailings
- ♦ To keep to scheduled sailing dates
- ♦ To fix the trade share for each member of the conference

The advantage of the conference system is that

- It allows members to adjust capacity to meet demand
- It guarantees a fixed freight rate
- It avoids inefficient duplication of port calls during the voyage by its members

There are about two hundred conferences worldwide, with fifteen being UK-based and twenty operating from the United States.

There is one unfortunate residual effect of the traditional conference systems. For being well established, they do tend to exclude new and developing states from participating in a trade, especially where the developing states are trying to initiate their own shipping lines from countries that are on an established conference line.

To overcome the reluctance of traditional maritime countries in allowing participation by the developing states, a conference was convened, under the auspices of the United Nations Conference on Trade and Development (UNCTAD), for an International Convention on a Code of Conduct for Liner Conference systems, often known by UNCTAD Liner Code or 40/40/20, which is the proportional share-out of seaborne trade between two participating countries.

Liner Service Contracts

For the liner service, the most common form of contract between the shipping company and the cargo owner is evidenced by a bill of lading or a liner service way bill.

Modern shipment, between freight forwarder and shipping line, is contracted by means of a combined transport document.

It is possible for the shipowner to release his ship for a period of time to another person/company, and in this case, the charterer can control the ship on a liner trade under

- Demise charter party
- Time charter party

Tramp Operations

With a few exceptions, everything that is not liner service is covered by tramp operations.

A ship on tramp operations will call at any port to carry whatever cargo is available.

Even where the ship operates on a regular run between oil field and refinery it comes under this category of trading.

For on this regular trade, the tanker displays a characteristic feature of tramp ship operations, which is the lack of a return cargo.

It is the absence of a regular or constant load/unload of cargo that identifies this type of trade and provides problems for the ship manager.

At all times, he must be calculating months ahead to optimize the use of his ships, a consignment to Antarctica may provide a good freight, but where would the ship need to go to pick up its subsequent cargo?

All calculations for the freight rates charged for cargo carried must be based on the mobilization charge to get the ship to the load port and the demobilization charge to cover the ship's costs after discharge.

Obtaining cargoes, negotiating freight, and preparing contracts is a full-time occupation, and a shipping company that is involved in a tramp ship operation will either have a department specifically designated for its cargo procurement operations or it will use the comprehensive services of a shipowner's broker.

Tramp operations cover most types of cargo, though some contracts will cover the occasional consignment of general cargo; the vast majority will be for the carriage of bulk cargoes

- ♦ Oil
- ♦ Grain
- ♦ Coal
- ♦ Chemicals
- ♦ Liquefied gases
- ♦ Metal ores, e.g., bauxite

Tramp Operation Contracts

Contracts for tramp operations will generally be

- Voyage charter party
- Contracts of affreightment

Passenger Ships

Passenger ships make up approximately 2 percent of the total world tonnage.

There are very few, if any, passenger ships that operate solely on a completely deep-sea liner service, that is, a regular and scheduled run between identified ports.

Certainly some of the cargo liner services are prepared to carry up to twelve passengers (then the passenger ship regulations have to be complied with), and indeed, this type of passenger arrangement can provide a lucrative addition to the ship's operating revenue.

In addition, a few passenger ship companies operate a system of carrying passengers across the Atlantic prior to the ship going on to a subsequent cruise.

Most large ocean-going passenger ships (class 1) operate on cruises, either warm weather or "interest" cruises to a specific location, e.g. Norwegian fjords, Antarctica, or the Galápagos Islands for the birds.

This category includes the vast majority of the 4,080 passenger ships that are registered throughout the world.

The ships that operate on short sea services are usually known as ferries, and they can be as diverse as the Renfrew Ferry, operating as an overgrown launch across the River Clyde that is designed to carry an ambulance and the pride of Dover, one of the most modern cross

(English) channel Ro-Ro ships that carries 2,290 passengers and 650 cars and the Philippines interisland services.

Other types of passenger ship include the casino boats out of Miami, the crew boats that run workers to oil platforms and rigs, and the hajj ships that carry the pilgrims to Mecca and are legislated for under the special trade passenger ship agreement 1971.

Passenger ships operating in international waters are expected to comply with the relevant legislation concerning safety and pollution, that is, SOLAS and MARPOL.

Passenger Contracts

International legislation exists for regulations covering the liabilities of shipowners regarding passengers and passengers' luggage (Athens Convention).

This will be incorporated into the tickets issued to passengers when the flag state has ratified the convention as will any national legislation relating to passengers rights to form the basis of the contract between the shipping company and the passenger.

Other Cargoes

The maritime industry is full of specialist companies that operate the unusual, and sometimes bizarre, type of ship.

Though this type of trade only makes up 10 percent of the world's shipping, it does include some important areas:

- Providing backup and support to the oil industry: supply ships, tugs, anchor handlers, crane barges, lay barges, survey ships, etc.
- Heavy lift cargo ships
- Providing and assisting port operations: dredgers, tugs, pilot ships, etc.

- Miscellaneous sea-going ships: icebreakers, weather ships, survey and research ships, cable layers, etc.
- Floating storage tanks, e.g., Sirri Island

Most of the specialized ships will be designed for a specific task, though very occasionally a supply ship is converted into a general cargo ship.

The specific task is catered for by applying to the design, and operation, of the ship the known requirements of the job.

Contracts

Contracts will invariably be by charter party, the more specialized the task, the longer, and/or the more expensive the charter party as the ship will probably have been commissioned with that job in mind.

Once the type of trade has been recognized by marketing and research, the shipowner will proceed with ship acquisition; how he does that will depend on the following:

- The trade: its continuity, volume and revenue generating possibilities
- The availability of adequate ships and the costs of operating them
- The possible exclusions enforced by other state legislation

Fixing a Cargo

A ship, not normally engaged in tramping, presently has a full cargo to be unloaded in Australia and a subsequent cargo waiting in Western Europe.

The shipowner would like a backhaul cargo from Australia to assist with his operating costs; therefore, he must enter the market to obtain a fixture for his ship.

As his in-house knowledge of possible cargoes, rates, and procedure will probably be limited, he must engage the services of an expert to find a cargo and do his negotiating; this is carried out on his behalf by an owner's broker.

The shipowner must advertise the fact that he is willing to carry cargo; he can either do this on a general level, if he has experience, by sending out a telex to known cargo exporters or chartering brokers that will arrange the entire contact and contract.

More likely, however, the shipowner will nominate an exclusive shipowner's broker to act for him, engaging him with a contract that details the extent of his responsibility and authority.

He will inform his broker that he has a ship available and furnish him with details of the ship

- Type of ship: Ro-Ro, general
- cargo, tanker
- Loading ability: cranes, no gear

When and where she will be

available: e.g., Australia

- Area of trade anticipated: e.g., Western Europe
- Carrying capacity: net tonnage,
- dimensions
- Any other relevant information
- Type of cargo: clean/dirty

It is possible that the shipowner will just ask for details of any cargo available; that will depend on how desperate he is to fix his ship.

When he receives these instructions, the broker will acquaint himself with the overall picture trade; he probably has a good idea of what is and what is not available already. This knowledge of what cargoes are available comes from using a clearing house of cargo information called a freight market; one of the better known is accommodated at the Baltic Exchange.

The Baltic Exchange

The Baltic Exchange Limited, to use its full title, is an institution located in the city of London. Approximately six hundred UK-registered companies of a wide variety of international ownership are members of the exchange, and they are engaged in many different activities connected with international trade

The *freight market* is the main activity of the members of the Baltic and covers the provision of shipping transport for bulk cargoes. As the information of ships and cargoes available is substantial, a degree of specialization is inevitable.

Every member involved in the freight market has to maintain a constant record of both the availability of ships and their locations, coupled with a knowledge of cargoes that are looking for carriage.

It is the duty of members of the freight market to match up the available ships and cargoes. When a cargo is identified, it is customary for the shipowner to make the initial offer; this offer will be sketchy and cover only the main elements of the eventual fixture.

- Cargo size and description
- Lay days and cancelling days
- Rate of freight
- Lay time allowed
- Demurrage/dispatch
- The title of the charter party he would like to use

The commission

With reference to these salient points, the questions for the shipowner and his broker at this stage are as follows:

- What rates do they tender? Do they offer more than what was last done? If so, how much more?
- Do they agree to the charterer's usual terms, if known?
- How badly is the business needed?

The first decision concerns the freight rate. This is something of an art as there is no known secret formula that calculates what is a good rate.

The situation in the market will have an effect on the rate and so will the attitude of the charterer and his broker. The rate will be determined by the knowledge, intuition, and downright nosiness of the shipowner's broker; how desperate the charterer is to fix a ship can be gleaned from the most unlikely sources!

Experience will show the broker how to handle the situation, and he will soon learn which owners have a reputation for always asking very high prices and then reducing and those whose initial offer is close to their fixing rate. Likewise he should soon learn the foibles of the charterers.

One reasonable way of ascertaining the going rate of freight is to consult daily and weekly trade periodicals, for example, *Fairplay*, for what rates ships have recently been fixed at; for tankers this is expressed at a new Worldscale rate.

New Worldscale Rate

The Worldwide Tanker Nominal Freight Scale, code name Worldscale, is a schedule of freight rates applying to tankers carrying oil cargoes in bulk. It is unique to tanker voyage chartering; no other sector of shipping uses such a system.

The word *nominal* needs to be noted because the freight rates that Worldscale provides are intended solely as a standard reference and comparison by means of which rates for all voyages and market levels can be compared and readily judged.

Basically Worldscale is a set of rates quoting the freight rate per tonne for each of a very large number of possible voyages.

In making the first offer, owners

- Need the highest possible freight rate consistent with the market to maximize earnings
- Require the best terms
- Must ensure that the first offer draws a counteroffer from the charterer in the knowledge that most negotiations fall at the first hurdle

At this point, it is worth mentioning that the prudent shipowner, and/or his broker, should keep a record of the details of all offers and counteroffers. A log of this sort is invaluable at a later date when some dispute arises over who said what and when.

Depending on what contract is being negotiated, an initial offer from the shipowner would be followed by a counteroffer by the charterer.

A straightforward one-commodity charter party, e.g., NORGRAIN, leaves little room for other negotiations, whereas Gen Con, which can be used to cover most cargoes and most voyages, allows additional clauses and can be made as complicated as both parties wish and can agree on. A tanker voyage charter party will involve the addition of "clauses" outlining the exact nature of the contract.

Once the contract is signed, it becomes binding on both parties, and the broker is paid his commission as agreed in the charter party.

Contracts of Carriage

Bill of Lading

The bill of lading is one of the most important documents related to the commercial operations of shipping.

Without the bill of lading, the international transport industry would not be as we know it today; in fact, international trade would probably not exist in its present guise, and cargo supernumeraries would have more power and authority than the ship's master.

The international, commercial movement of cargo needs the bill of lading.

- It provides the wherewithal to allow cargo to be bought and sold when the parties to the transaction are separated by thousands of miles.
- It allows goods to be transferred between owners while the goods are still being carried on a ship.
- It provides security for bank loans and mortgages.
- It provides persons not party to the original sale with rights and obligations regarding the transport of the goods, their loss, damage, or destruction.
- It provides a detailed description of the goods and the conditions in which it was loaded.

Unfortunately, the bill of lading can also be abused (see maritime crime).

The bill of lading's identity and legal standing is provided for by national and international law, by case law and precedent, and by common usage over many years.

International Law

Conventions for the unification of certain rules of law relating to the 1924 Bills of Lading (Hague Rules) and the 1968 protocol, which collectively make up the Hague-Visby Rules, are the main regulations that influence the format, issue, and use of bills of lading.

There is a lesser used Convention on the Carriage of Goods by Sea (1978) sponsored by UNCTAD and known as the Hamburg Rules that is supposed to eventually replace the Hague and Hague-Visby Rules.

However, there is much-entrenched feeling against the Hamburg Rules from the traditional maritime industry as it places a greater burden of responsibility on the carrier, that is, ship, than the more widely used Hague/Hague-Visby.

National Law

Most maritime states have some form of national legislation based on the minimum requirements of Hague/Hague-Visby; the United States has the Carriage of Goods by Sea Act (1936), which uses the Hague Rules, and the United Kingdom has the COGSA (1971), which follows Hague-Visby.

The bill of lading has three main functions:

- Receipt of goods shipped
- Good evidence of contract
- Document of title

And these functions give the bill of lading its importance in the aspects of ship operations.

- As a receipt of goods loaded, the bill of lading provides an exact assessment as to the quantity or weight of the commodity, its condition on loading, and even its value.
- The bill of lading also provides the name of the ship and its owner and where and when goods were loaded.
- As a document of title, the bill of lading allows the lawful possessor of the bill to be considered the lawful owner of the cargo described on it.

Thus transferring the bill of lading between seller and buyer is akin to transferring the rights of property in the goods themselves.

- Good evidence of contract is important because subsequent buyers of the described cargo will not have been parties to the original contract of affreightment and will not be aware of the rights and obligations of that contract. Thus, the bill of lading's clauses and conditions will be those that are applicable between the carrier (ship) and the owner of the cargo.

Once the goods have been loaded, the bill of lading is given to the shipper by the captain of the carrying ship.

The shipper can either

- Transfer the goods to the intended buyer by exchanging the bill of lading for money, usually through an intermediary, e.g., a bank
- Put the goods on the open market, selling them to whoever offers the most money

In the first instance, it will probably be the case that the seller and the buyer of the goods have conducted a contract of sale on some previous occasion, and the transfer of the bill of lading will be the completion of that contract.

In the second instance, the shipper, a cargo trader, will have bought and shipped the goods as a speculative venture, with no positive knowledge of the identity of the final purchaser of the goods, and during the passage of the cargo, it will change hands any number of times before it arrives at its destination. Some oil cargoes are known to have been bought and sold as many as 100–150 times during the course of its carriage from the Gulf and Western Europe.

The importance of the bill of lading now becomes evident.

- *Document of title.* The buyer of the goods does not necessarily have to see them as exchange of bill of lading is sufficient for the transfer of the goods.
- *Receipt of goods shipped.* The buyer knows the condition of the goods is correct from what is described on the bill of lading.
- *Good evidence of contract.* The buyer, many times removed from the original contractors of shipper and carrier, can see from the bill of lading what terms cover the contract. He also knows the bill of lading is governed by Hague, Hague-Visby, or Hamburg Rules (or their national equivalent) and that the terms and conditions of the contract must be reasonable

Though the traditional "shipped" bill of lading is the most widely used method in the carriage of sea cargoes, there are other cargo documents that are growing in popularity.

- *Waybill.* Sometimes known as a container bill, it has the functions of a traditional bill with regard to good evidence and receipt of goods, but it is not transferable as the cargo must be discharged to the consignee, whose name is included on the waybill.
- *Combined bill of lading.* With the advent of multimodal transport, road-ship-road, the identity of the contracting carrying party could be in doubt; therefore, this type of document allows the combined transport operator (see freight forwarder) to assume responsibility for the care of the cargo, irrespective of which actual carrier damages, delays, or loses the goods and disregarding which form of transport was being used at the time of the loss.

Authorization to Sign Bills of Lading

Under a time or voyage charter party, the master in signing bills of lading acts as agent for shipowner. Similarly, if a loading broker or charterers' agent signs bills of lading, it will be as agent of the shipowner. However, both time and voyage charter parties often contain a demise clause, which will state whether the master or another is signing on behalf of the owner or the charterer.

Under the terms of many time charter parties and some voyage charter parties, the owners transfer the authority to sign bills of lading to the charterers, thereby canceling the authority normally held by the master. In these circumstances, the master should not sign bills of lading and cannot delegate authority to others to do so. If in doubt, however, he should request specific instructions first from his owners and secondly from the time charterers. If the time charterers tell the master to do nothing, they have retained their own authority to sign bills of lading. If they instruct him to authorize a named agent, they have, in doing so, passed their own authority back to the master.

In any case in which the agent will be signing bills of lading on behalf of the master, the master should ensure that the agent receives appropriate instructions in the form of an authorization which he should issue. The wording of any such authorization is often dictated by owners' or charterers' voyage instructions, and the master should consult his owner if he is in any doubt as to the form of instruction to be issued.

The authorization should be given to the agent, and a copy should be retained by the master with the agent's signed acknowledgment.

It is common practice for agents to present masters with letters of authority that are worded to the agent's own advantage. The master is never obliged to use such forms. He can always use the owners' wording. If such agents refuse to accept such an authority, the master should inform owners and time charterers accordingly.

In some trades, such as the grain and agricultural products trades, it is common to have thirty to forty bills of lading. In these circumstances, it is advisable for the master, always acting under instructions, to delegate his authority to one or several named individuals in the agency and to obtain copies of their signatures on all copies of the letter of authority. This will help to reduce opportunity for fraud when bills of lading are presented to the master at the discharge port. It is important to stress that the master should always be aware of the precise terms of any relevant charter party clauses and should consult his owners if he is in any doubt as to the existence or extent of his authority to sign bills of lading, whether on behalf of owners or charterers.

Before signing the bill of lading, the master should ensure that

1. The goods are actually aboard and the bill of lading is correctly dated
2. The description of the goods complies with the mate's receipts, failing which the bill of lading should be claused accordingly. If he doubts about clausing the bill of lading, he should consult his owners, some of whom will refer him to the local P & I club representative while others consider this too important a matter for anyone but themselves.
3. That he only ever signs the same number of originals as is shown on the face of the bill of lading. If three originals are shown on the document, as is usual, only three should be signed.

4. The bill of lading contains a clause referring to any relevant charter party and includes the protection clauses specified in that charter party. Very specific wording is often required in order to achieve the protection of all relevant charter party provisions, and the master should consult his owners. However, the master is usually required to sign bills of lading as presented, and there is little that he can do except bring the matter to the notice of owners and charterers if the bills of lading do not contain the specific clauses.

The master should not

1. Sign a bill of lading which is in any respect inaccurate.
2. Be persuaded to sign clean bills of lading against the offer of a letter of indemnity.
3. Sign bills of lading which name a destination which is outside the range named in the charter party or in the voyage orders or which the vessel cannot physically reach. He must not sign a bill of lading which explicitly forbids transshipment if the vessel's draft will make transshipment unavoidable.

Payment of Freight

A bill of lading which contains no reference to freight having been paid in whole or in part is a receipt only for cargo, but a bill of lading marked "freight paid" or "freight prepaid" may be a receipt for both cargo and freight money.

The master should only sign "freight paid" or "freight prepaid" B/L, where he is specifically instructed to do so by owners (but not by charterers), or he is specifically instructed to do so by time charterers if the charter party allows them to do so, or the charter party explicitly requires him to do so, or he has good evidence that the freight has indeed been properly paid and received by owners or time charterers, but this should always be checked.

If none of the above conditions is satisfied, the master should delete the words "freight paid" or "freight prepaid" and should initial this amendment before signing. If this proves impossible, the master should pass the bill of lading to the agent with a written instruction not to issue it without explicit instructions from his owners and should notify owners of what he has done. It should be noted that voyage charterers cannot insist on a "freight paid" bill of lading being signed before payment of freight unless the charter party explicitly allows it. In any event the position should be checked. Signature of "freight paid" bills of lading in a situation where freight had not in fact been paid may lead to the loss of the owner's right later to exercise a lien for unpaid freight.

Time charterers can insist on a "freight prepaid" bill of lading being signed provided that the charter party specifically allows them to do so, but the master should assume that they do not want such a bill of lading signed unless they have given him specific instructions to sign.

General Considerations at Time of Sailing from the Load Port

On no account should the master sail without either issuing a bill of lading under his own signature or else delegating the signing to the agent. On sailing from the load port, the master should notify the discharge port agents that he will require to see original bills of lading for the cargo before he will authorize its discharge, and he should insist that they acknowledge and confirm his instructions in writing, unless owners have instructed him in writing that they consider this procedure unnecessary.

If the master should at any time discover that he has issued an incorrect bill of lading, he must notify owners immediately, giving full details of its particulars, including names of shippers and consignees. He must also notify those parties.

Delivery of Cargo in Return for Bill of Lading

When the ship has arrived in the discharge port, the cargo must be safely discharged into the care of the correct person.

When the cargo has been received aboard ship and the master has issued a bill of lading in respect of it, he becomes responsible for ensuring that it is delivered to those whom he reasonably believes to be entitled to its possession. The master should only give delivery of cargo against production of one of the three original bills of lading or under specific instructions from owners. It is extremely bad practice to assume that the agent has attended to this matter on owner's behalf, as this is often not the case.

The master should give plenty of advance warning to the discharging port agent that he will require to see the original bills of lading. This ensures that the agent has time in which to arrange to comply.

When original bills of lading have not reached the discharge port the owners may agree to discharge the cargo against letters of indemnity provided by the receivers, shippers or charterers, but that is a decision for the owners and not for the master. When the owners instruct the master to accept a letter of indemnity (LOI), they will take steps to ensure that the wording of the LOI presented to the master is the same as that which they have proposed. The master should then check carefully that the LOI presented matches the one supplied to him by owners.

Proper delivery of cargo against bill of lading

There are three situations in which the master must be particularly alert to ensure the proper delivery of the cargo. These are change of destination, transshipment/lightering, and split bills of lading and/or part cargoes.

Change of destination. If the master receives an instruction to proceed to some port or place other than the one that appears in the bill of lading, he should draw this fact to the attention of all concerned as soon as possible. This rule applies regardless of whether the instruction comes from owners, time charterers, voyage charterers, or agents.

There is no P & I cover for misdelivery of cargo, so change of destination is usually the subject of a letter of indemnity (LOI). Provided that the change of destination is confirmed, the master should contact the agent at the new destination to ensure that he has in his possession at least one original bill of lading. Although this document names the original destination, it will still be delivered to the master and accomplished in the normal way, provided that the LOI has been issued and accepted by the owner. The owner will retain the LOI.

Transshipment/lightening. On receiving the instructions to transship or lighten all or part of his cargo, the master should always ask himself whether this instruction is consistent with the bill of lading. If it is not, he must immediately notify all concerned.

On parting with all or part of his vessel's cargo other than at its final destination, the master should ensure that he receives a clean and plainly worded receipt for it, signed by a qualified person such as the master or chief mate of the other vessel. The master should ensure that the receipt states the full quantity transferred, this being particularly important in the case of part discharge or lightening, as if the vessel has actually discharged more cargo than stated in the receipt, there will be a shortage at the next port.

Split bill of lading and/or part cargoes. There are two types of split bill of lading. The first occurs where a consignment of cargo described in one bill of lading is split at the discharge port and sold partly to one receiver and partly to another. In these circumstances, delivery is given against delivery orders to which all the conditions of the original bills of lading apply. Usually, the required number of delivery orders is issued by the owner's agent when all the original copies of the bill of lading are presented to him. The master will give delivery of the cargo against production of all the originals plus all the delivery orders. Delivery orders are made out in original only, with no copies, and are often unacceptable to banks, which severely limit their use.

More difficult is the situation in which the charterers require bills of lading for several parcels of cargo when the master originally issued a single set of bills of lading for the entire consignment. For example, it might be that one set of bills of lading was issued for the entire cargo, but the charterers and their traders require three sets of bill of lading, each for one-third of total cargo. This differs from the first case because three sets of negotiable bills of lading are required. The procedure for dealing with this is simple in theory and difficult in practice. The one set of originals is collected and delivered to the owners or their nominated agents, together with the required number of replacements. The owners destroy the original set and sign and issue the replacement sets. If the master is requested to authorize the issuing of split bills of lading, he should refer the matter to owners and await orders.

Contracts of Sale

The contract between the cargo seller and the cargo buyer is a contract for the sale of goods and is normally quite separate from the ship's charter or other contract of carriage. Certain aspects of the sale of goods contract are important for a shipmaster to understand.

Contract for sale of goods have three important points:

- The time or circumstances of the *passing of ownership* of the goods from seller to buyer,
- The time *when payment becomes due*, and
- The time *when the risk (of loss/damage) passes* from seller to buyer.

International sale of goods contracts usually incorporate a set of mutually agreed trade terms named incoterms, which help the buyer and seller avoid misunderstanding over the above points.

FOB and CIF are the chief incoterms used for sea or inland waterway transport.

All that concerns the shipowner is that somebody wishes him to carry goods; this could be either the purchaser when the contact of sale will be FOB or the seller when the contract of sale will be CIF.

The respective purchaser or seller will enter into a contract with the shipowner to carry the goods.

Free on Board (FOB)

The seller of the goods must supply the goods and documents stated in the contract of sale.

He must load the goods on board the vessel named by buyer at the named port of shipment on the date or within the period stipulated.

The seller must bear all costs and risks of the goods until they have passed the ship's rail at the named port of shipment, including export charges and taxes.

He must also pay for packing where necessary. Risk passes when the goods pass the ship's rail. The seller must notify the buyer when the goods have been loaded.

The buyer charters a ship or reserves the necessary space on a ship and notifies the seller of the ship's name, loading berth, and loading dates.

The buyer bears all costs, including insurance (which he must arrange) and freight, from the time the goods cross the ship's rail at loading port, from when he is liable to pay the contract price. (freight is normally collectable by the carrier from the buyer at the discharge port.) The buyer must also pay the seller for providing the required documents, e.g. Bills of lading and certificate of origin. The seller must give sufficient information to the buyer for him to arrange insurance. If the seller fails to give enough information, the risk stays with him.

Cost, Insurance, Freight (CIF)

Cost, Insurance, Freight is the name given to a contract of sale where the buyer of the goods is quoted a price that covers all the expenses of getting the goods from the seller to a place nominated by the buyer, where he can claim possession of them.

The seller of the goods is responsible for contracting and paying for a contract of carriage with the shipowner, delivering the cargo to the loading port, and paying all expenses for the loading of the vessel.

The buyer of the goods is only responsible for nominating the discharge port, paying for the goods, and taking delivery.

Normally, payment is made by the buyer when he receives the bill of lading for the goods, and he is aware that the cargo is being "shipped" to his nominate port of discharge.

The seller is also bound to arrange the insurance of the cargo through a responsible underwriter and attend to the requirements of export licenses, permits, and clearance.

Hague and Hague-Visby Rules

In 1924, the first international attempt at the codification and unification of rules concerning bills of lading and the carriage of goods by sea was completed in a convention known as the Hague Rules.

By the end of the 1960s, it was realized that the original rules were dated and inadequate for modern usage, and a new conference was convened to agree on a protocol that would bring the rules some way toward the contemporary practice of carriage of goods by sea.

The original rules that now include the changes brought about by the protocol are known as the Hague-Visby Rules (1968).

This section deals with the complete Hague-Visby rules that are found as the schedule in the United Kingdom's Carriage of Goods by Sea Act 1971 (COGSA 71). All references to the original convention, where it differs from Hague-Visby, will be in italics, sections of Hague-Visby that were not included in the original rules are underlined.

Hague-Visby Rules

The rules consist of ten articles that include the rights, immunities, responsibilities and liabilities of carriers, shippers and endorsees who enter into a contract of carriage of goods.

The contract is in relation to the loading, handling, stowage, carriage, custody, care, and discharge of goods (art. 2).

Carrier includes the owner or the charterer who enters into a contract of carriage with a shipper (art. 1 (a)).

"Contract of carriage" applies only to contracts of carriage covered by a bill of lading or any similar document of title, where they are issued (art. I (b)) or where the shipper can demand that they be issued (art. III (3); (*Harland and Wolff v. Burns and Laird Lines* (1944)).

This can include a bill of lading issued under a charter party from the moment at which the bill of lading regulates the relations between the carrier and the holder of the bill of lading, i.e., when it is transferred by the charterer to a third party.

"Goods" include goods, wares, merchandise, and articles of every kind whatsoever *except live animals and cargo which by contract is stated as being carried on deck and is so carried* (art. I (c)).

"Carriage of goods" covers the period from the time when the goods are loaded on to the time they are discharged from the ship (art. I (e)), provided that the ports of loading and discharge are in two different states (art. X), and the port from which carriage is made or from where the bill of lading is issued is in a contracting state; i.e., the state has ratified the convention and protocol (art. X).

This applies whatever the nationality of the ship, the carrier, the shipper, the consignee, or other interested persons (art. X).

The rules apply during the loading and unloading operations.

"Loaded on" is interpreted as being the beginning of the operation of loading the goods of the shipper concerned and not as the moment when the goods in question cross the ship's rail. Where the loading of the shipper's goods has begun and some of the goods which have not yet been loaded are damaged before they have crossed the ship's rail, the liability for this damage is governed by Hague-Visby Rules.

Obligations under the HVRs

There are three basic carrier's obligations under the Hague-Visby Rules (HVRs):

- To ensure the vessel's seaworthiness,
- To look after the cargo, and
- To issue a B/L.

Obligation under the HVRs in Respect of Seaworthiness

Under article III (1) and IV (1), the carrier must, before and at the beginning of the voyage (i.e., up to the moment of sailing), to exercise *due diligence* to

- Make the ship seaworthy,
- Properly man, equip, and supply the ship, and
- Make the holds, refrigerating, and cool chambers and all other parts of the ship in which goods are carried fit and safe for their reception, carriage, and preservation.

Due diligence means taking all reasonable precautions to see that the vessel is fit for the voyage contemplated. The carrier is not obliged to give an absolute guarantee of seaworthiness. The carrier may delegate his duty to exercise due diligence (e.g., to surveyors or repairers), but he will be responsible if they fail to exercise due diligence in carrying out their work.

Seaworthy, in this context, means that the hull must be in sound condition; the vessel must be mechanically sound, equipped with charts, etc., and crewed by a properly trained crew. The holds must be fit and safe for the reception, carriage and preservation of the cargo, and in particular, the hatch covers must be tight, and there must be no instability of the vessel through improper stowage. It has been held that the neglect to protect a water pipe in a hold from frost, which could have been expected at the time of the year showed a lack of due diligence to make the vessel seaworthy.

The vessel need only be seaworthy at the commencement of the voyage, which usually means when she leaves the berth, whether under her own motive power or with the aid of tugs.

If a cargo owner can show that his loss was caused by a failure of the carrier to exercise due diligence to make the vessel seaworthy, the carrier will not be able to rely on any other clauses in the rules which reduce his liability (i.e., the exceptions to liability).

Obligation under the HVRs toward the Cargo

The carrier must *"properly and carefully load, handle, stow, carry, keep, care for and discharge any goods carried."*
Unlike seaworthiness, this duty extends throughout the voyage and implies greater care than "due diligence." The courts do not expect perfection from the carrier, but it has been held that stowage was improper where

- Contamination of other goods occurred;
- There was inadequate or no ventilation;
- Dry cargo was damaged by liquid goods; and
- Vehicles were secured only by their own brakes.

The carrier must have a sound system for looking after the cargo when stowed. He has a duty to use all reasonable means to ascertain the nature and characteristics of the cargo and to care for it accordingly though the shipper should give special instructions where special care is required. (Where water in tractor radiators froze, it was held that the carrier should have been told of the risk.)

Obligation under HVRs to Issue a B/L

After receiving the goods into his charge, the carrier shall, on demand of the shipper, issue to the shipper a bill of lading, showing among other things, the following:

- All leading marks for identification of the goods, as stated by the shipper before loading (in his shipping note or boat note), provided these are visible on the goods or their coverings;
- Either the number of packages or pieces, or quantity, or weight, as stated by the shipper (in his shipping note or boat note); and
- The apparent order and condition of the goods.

These details will provide prima facie evidence of receipt of cargo in the manner and condition so described (art. III (4)).

Thus, the carrier, master or agent, is allowed to state or show in the bill of lading any marks, number, quantity, or weight that he has reasonable grounds for suspecting not accurately represent the goods actually received (art. III (3)). This makes the "clean" bill of lading a "dirty" bill of lading.

When the goods are eventually removed into the custody of the consignee, the details on the bill of lading are prima facie evidence of the condition of the goods on discharge, unless

a. Notice of loss or damage has been given in writing to the carrier before or at the time of the removal.
b. Such notice is given within three (3) days when the loss or damage is not apparent (article III (6)).

The carrier and the ship shall be in any event be discharged from all liability whatsoever in respect of the goods, unless suit is brought within one (1) year of their delivery or of the date when they should have been delivered (art. III (6)).

This paragraph must be complied with, or the goods owner will lose the chance to bring a case against the carrier.

The word *suit* also includes arbitration.

An action for indemnity against a third person may be brought even after the expiration of the year provided if brought within the time allowed by the court involved with the case (article III (6 bis)).

Article III (7) continues with the practical application of issuing "shipped" bills of lading on the surrender of other documents of title.

Any clause, covenant, or agreement in a contract of carriage relieving the carrier or the ship from liability for loss or damage to, or in connection with, goods arising from negligence, fault, or failure in the duties and obligations provided in the article III, or lessening such liability shall be null and void and of no effect (article III (8)).

Exclusion of Liability

Article IV provides the rules with the extent to which the carrier can exclude or limit his liability.

The carrier and the ship cannot be responsible for loss or damage arising or resulting from the following:

   a. Act, neglect, or default of the master, mariner, pilot, or the servants of the carrier in the navigation or in the management of the ship (art. IV, 2 (a)).

"Management of ship" is construed as meaning acts which were wholly or primarily done with the object of managing the ship herself as opposed to the cargo.

Management of the ship means "management of the ship . . . and not . . . the general carrying on of the business of transporting goods by sea."

   b. Fire, unless caused by the actual fault or privity of the carrier (art. IV, 2 (b)).

This section affords no protection if the fire was caused by unseaworthiness.

   c. Perils, dangers, and accidents of the sea or other navigable waters (art. IV, 2 (c)).

This includes pirates, but on a more mundane level, it also includes losses not peculiar to the sea, like rats or cockroaches eating goods in a ship, as well as sea-related losses, such as foundering after a collision.

In recent cases, courts have accepted that the entry of sea water was a peril of the sea; however, the weather has to be abnormal for it to apply.

> d. Act of God (art. IV, 2 (d)). "The act of God is a mere short way of expressing this proposition: A carrier is not liable for any accident as to which he can show that it is due to natural causes, directly and exclusively, without human intervention, and that it could not have been prevented by any amount of foresight and pains and care reasonably to be expected of him" (*Nugent v. Smith* (1876)).

It can include the following:

> i. A sudden gust of wind
> ii. Fall of rain heavier than any within living memory
> iii. A ship encountering more than ordinary weather
>
> e. Act of war (article IV, 2 (e)).
> f. Act of public enemies (article IV, 2 (f)). This phrase is also interpreted as "King or Queen's enemies"; it does not include robbers on land, but it can include pirates, as robbers at sea, as being enemies of all nations.

The master is justified in putting into port and delaying the voyage where he has a reasonable apprehension of danger from capture by an "enemy of the King/Queen."

> g. Arrest or restraint of princes, rulers or people, or seizure under legal process (article 2 (g)).

This section covers any forcible interference with the voyage or the venture at the hands of the constituted government or ruling power of any country.

It includes the following: (i) orders of government prohibiting or restricting the exportation or landing of goods and (ii) embargo.

- h. Quarantine restrictions (article IV, 2 (h))
- i. Act or omission of the shipper or owner of the goods, his agent or representative (article IV, 2 (i))
- j. Strikes or lockouts or stoppages or restraint of labor from whatever cause, whether partial or general (article IV, 2 (j))
- k. Riots and civil commotions (article IV, 2 (k))
- l. Saving or attempting to save life or property at sea (article IV, 2 (l)).

This is allowed where it does not extend beyond the necessity of the particular case.

- m. Wastage in bulk or weight or any other loss or damage arising from inherent defect, quality or vice of the goods (article IV, 2 (m))—wastage includes leakage.

Inherent vice or defect is a defect in the goods carried that is incidental to the nature of the things themselves.

Vice "is not a moral vice, but is the sort which by its internal development tends to the destruction or the injury of the animal or thing to be carried."

Inherent vice does not cover goods that were stowed incorrectly and thus were damaged.

- n. Insufficiency of packing (article IV, 2 (n)). Where the carrier has issued a clean bill of lading for goods shipped, he will not be able to rely on this exception if the insufficiency of packaging was externally visible on a reasonable examination on shipment.
- o. Insufficiency or inadequacy of marks (article IV, 2 (o)).

Generally, this exception only excuses the carrier from delivering the actual goods shipped if he can prove the following:

i. That the goods are unidentifiable owing to insufficiency of marks and
ii. That he has not lost any of them or, if he has, that they were lost by some other excepted peril

The exception will not cover the cases where marks are incorrect (as compared with the stated marks on the bill of lading) or inaccurate.

p. Latent defects not discoverable by due diligence (article IV, 2 (p)).

This section refers to latent defects that can occur in the ship, as with the hull, machinery, and appurtenances. A "latent defect" is any defect that is not apparent and cannot be discovered by due diligence.

Under English law, if the latent defect is not discoverable by due diligence, the carrier is apparently not liable even if he failed to exercise due diligence in attempting to discover latent defects.

q. Any other cause arising without the actual fault or privity of the carrier, or without the fault or neglect of the agents or servants of the carrier (but the burden of proof shall be on the person claiming the benefit of this exception to show that neither the actual fault or privity of the carrier nor the fault or neglect of the agents or servants of the carrier contributed to the loss or damage) (article IV, 2 (q)).

Deviation under the HVRs

Any deviation in saving or attempting to save life or property at sea or any reasonable deviation shall not be deemed to be an infringement or breach of the rules or of any contract of carriage. Thus, the carrier shall not be liable for any loss or damage resulting from the "reasonable deviation" (article IV (4)).

The question as to what is a reasonable deviation for the purposes of article IV (4) is probably a matter of fact in every case.

It must be

   a. Limited to departures from the route that were in the contemplation of the parties at the time the contract was made.
   b. It must be reasonable to all the parties concerned, not just from the point of view of the carrier or that of the cargo owner concerned in the dispute, but of all the cargo owners.

It was further held that a deviation in the national interest would be justified, but not to land shore workers.

Under this section, there may be a duty to deviate to safeguard the cargo, where it is perishable and cannot be discharged at a strike-bound port.

Dangerous Goods under HVRs

The HVRs provide that inflammable, explosive, or dangerous goods that have been shipped without the consent of the carrier, master or agent (or without their knowledge of the nature and character of the goods), may at any time before discharge

- Be landed at any place,
- Be destroyed, or
- Be rendered innocuous by the carrier.

No compensation is payable, and the shipper of the goods will be liable for all damages and expenses directly or indirectly arising out of or resulting from the shipment.

If any such goods, legally shipped with the knowledge and consent of the carrier, master or agent, become a danger to the ship or other cargo, they may similarly be landed at any place, destroyed, or rendered innocuous by the carrier without liability on any part of the carrier except to general average, if any.

Limitation of Liability

Unless the nature and the value of the goods have been declared by the shipper before shipment and inserted in the bill of lading, neither the carrier nor the ship shall be liable for any loss or damage to, or in connection with the goods that exceeds the amount of

a. 666.67 units of account per package or unit or
b. 2 units of account per kilo of gross weight of goods lost or damaged, whichever is higher (article IV, 5 (a)).

The maximum amount payable may be raised by agreement between the carrier and the shipper (article IV, 5 (g)).

The "unit of account" is a Special Drawing Right (SDR) as defined by the International Monetary Fund (IMF) (article IV, 5(d)).

The value of the SDR is £1 = 1.29339 SDR $1 = 0.76850 SDR (August 1988); these values vary only slightly over a period of time.

The actual wording of the 1968 protocol is 10,000 francs per package and 30 francs per kilo, with the "franc" being defined as 65.5 milligrams of gold of millesimal fineness 900. However, this has all been updated by a further protocol of 1979.

Under the 1921 Hague Rules, the maximum amount was £100 per package or unit or the equivalent of that sum in other currency; however, it was possible to raise this maximum by agreement between the shipper and the carrier.

Package or unit under the Hague Rules caused some concern; a railway wagon was a "package," but unboxed cars were not.

As vessels became palletized and containerized, the problems grew (pallets of six cartons a "package") and even exist in the United States (a nonsignatory to Hague-Visby) post-Hague-Visby (350 adding machines in one container).

The problem of goods consolidated into containers, pallets, or other similar articles of transport has been rectified by Hague-Visby Rules:

- "The number of packages or units enumerated in the bill of lading as packed in such article of transport shall be deemed the number of packages or units for the purpose" of these rules (article IV, 5 (c)).
- Packages must have its ordinary meaning and cartons of color television sets inside the containers were to be considered "packages."
- However, when there is no mention of internal packages, the article of transport is to be considered the package or unit (article IV, 5 (c)).
- The total value recoverable is calculated by reference to the value of the goods at the place and time at which the goods are discharged from the ship or by the commodity exchange price (article IV, 5 (b)).
- Article IV bis is completely unique to the Hague-Visby Rules; it provides the defenses that are available under the Himalaya clause, in as much as that it applies the limitation of liability to the servants and agents of the carrier, enabling such individuals, if sued personally, to claim the benefits of the Rules as far as limitation of liability and defenses to an action are concerned. The action can be in contract or tort (article IV bis (1)).
- The Article IV bis does not cover "independent contractors."
- The carrier has the liberty to surrender all or part of his rights or immunities or to increase any of his responsibilities and obligations under these Rules (article V).

Special Agreements

Where particular goods are to be carried, the carrier, agent or master, and the shipper may enter into any agreement, in any terms as to responsibilities and liability, as far as the stipulations are not contrary to public policy or the care and diligence of the carriers servants or agents in regard to loading, handling, stowage, carriage, custody, care, and discharge of the goods carried by sea.

Provided that this section shall not apply to ordinary commercial shipments made in the ordinary course of trade but only to other shipments where the character or condition of the property to be carried or circumstances, terms and conditions under which the carriage is to be performed are such as reasonably to justify a special agreement.

It is a further stipulation that there has been nor shall there be any bill of lading issued and the terms agreed shall be embodied in a receipt which shall be a nonnegotiable document and shall be marked as such. Article VI public policy refers only to agreements as to the carrier's obligation regarding seaworthiness.

The Hague-Visby Rules do not prevent an agreement between the carrier and shipper for custody, care, or handling of cargo before loading on and subsequent to discharge from the ship on which the goods are carried by sea; this provides agreements "through bills of lading" and "combined transport operations" (article VII).

The provisions of the Hague-Visby Rules do not affect the rights and obligations of the carrier, given by any national statute that is in force, which relates to the limitation of the liability of owners of seagoing vessels (article VIII).

The rules shall not affect the provisions of any international convention.

Convention Countries

Hague Rules

Algeria, Angola, Antigua, Argentina, Bahamas, Belize, Bolivia, Cuba, Cyprus, Dominican Republic, Fiji, Gambia, Ghana, Grenada, Guyana, Iran, Ireland, Israel, Ivory Coast, Jamaica, Kiribati, Kuwait, Madagascar, Malaysia, Monaco, Mozambique, Nauru, New Zealand, Paraguay, Peru, Portugal, Saint Kitts, Saint Lucia, Saint Vincent and Grenadines, Seychelles, Solomon Islands, Somalia, Taiwan, Trinidad and Tobago, Turkey, Tuvalu, USA (42 countries)

Hague-Visby Rules

Aruba, Australia, Belgium, Canada, China, Denmark, Ecuador, Egypt*, Finland, France, Germany, Greece, India, Italy, Japan, Netherlands, Norway, Papua New Guinea, Poland, Singapore, South Africa, South Korea, Spain, Sri Lanka, Sweden, Switzerland, Syria, Tonga, United Kingdom (29 Countries)

Hamburg Rules

Barbados, Botswana, Burkina Faso, Chile, Egypt*, Guinea, Hungary, Kenya, Lebanon, Lesotho, Malawi, Morocco, Nigeria, Romania, Senegal, Sierra Leone, Tanzania, Tunisia, Uganda, Zambia (20 Countries)

Hamburg Rules

The United Nations Convention on the Carriage of Goods by Sea 1978 were developed by UNCITRAL to replace the Hague and Hague-Visby Rules after complaints by shippers in developing countries that the existing Rules unfairly protected the ship owner and were too onerous for the shipper.

The Hamburg Rules clearly define the role of the carrier:

- Any person by whom or in whose name a contract of carriage of goods by sea has been concluded with a shipper and the actual carrier:
- Any person to whom the performance of the carriage of goods, or any part of the carriage, has been entrusted by the carrier (article 1).

The term *goods* includes live animals and where the goods are consolidated in a container, pallet, or similar article of transport; goods include such article of transport (article 1).

The convention is applicable for contracts of carriage by sea between two different states (article 2).

They are not applicable to charter parties. However, when a bill of lading is issued in pursuance with a charter party, the convention applies to a bill of lading when it governs the relationship between the carrier and the holder of the bill of lading who is not the charterer (article 2.3).

Bill of lading means a document that evidences a contract of carriage by sea and the taking over or loading of the goods by the carrier, and by which the carrier undertakes to deliver the goods against surrender of the document (article 1.7).

When the carrier takes the goods in his charge, he must, on demand of the shipper, issue to the shipper a bill of lading (article 14.1).

The contents of the bill of lading must include details of the cargo and its apparent condition, of the carrier and the shipper (article 15).

After the goods are loaded on board, the carrier must issue a "shipped" bill of lading to a shipper; the "shipped" bill of lading will state that the goods are on board a named ship and the date of loading. If the carrier has previously issued another document to the shipper, the shipper is to exchange it for the "shipped" bill of lading or is to have the original document amended to that of a "shipped" bill of lading (article 15.2).

The responsibility of the carrier for the goods covers the period during which the carrier is in charge of the goods at the port of loading during the voyage and at the port of discharge (article 4).

During this period, the carrier is liable for loss resulting from loss or damage to the goods as well as from delay in delivery, unless the carrier proves that he took all measures that could reasonably be required to avoid the occurrence and its consequences (article 5).

If the carrier is liable for loss or damage, he can limit his liability to 835 units of account per package or 2.5 units of account per kilogram, whichever is highest (article 6). The unit of account is a SDR (article 26).

The liability for delay is limited to two and half times the freight payable for the goods delayed but not exceeding the total freight payable under the contract of carriage of goods by sea (article 6).

The carrier is not entitled to limit his liability if it is proved that the loss, damage, or delay was caused by an act or omission done with intent or with the knowledge that such results would probably result (article 8).

The carrier is entitled to carry goods on deck only if such carriage is in accordance with an agreement with the shipper or with the usage of the particular trade or is required by statutory rules or regulations (article 9).

Article 10 makes the carrier responsible for the entire carriage whether or not he entrusts the carriage to an actual carrier (article 10).

Notice of loss or damage must be given in writing to the carrier not later than the working day after the day when the goods were handed over to the consignee. When loss or damage is not apparent, the notice in writing must be given within fifteen days of the handing over to the consignee (article 19.1 and 2).

No compensation shall be payable for loss resulting from delay in delivery unless a notice has been given in writing to the carrier within sixty days after the day when the goods were handed over to the consignee (article 19.5).

Any action relating to the carriage of goods is time barred if proceedings have not been instituted within a period of two years (article 20).

Charter Parties

Charter parties can be divided into two main categories:

- Demise
- Not by Demise

Demise Charter

The shipowner is paid to relinquish complete control of his ship to another company.

The law on demise charter parties (the most common of which is the bareboat charter) has been long established in that the charter party by way of demise is a lease of the ship where the charterer, not the owner, has possession of the ship in law (*Baumwoll v. Gilchrist* (1892)). The responsibility for the ship and its safe operation usually lies with the demise charterer.

Once the demise charterer obtains the ship, he will then operate it either himself or perhaps, to complicate matters, through a ship management agreement.

Not by Demise

Charter parties that are not by demise can be divided into the following classes.

The shipowner is paid for the use of his vessel and retains some degree of control over its operation.

This area of charter parties can be subdivided into:

- Time Charter
- Voyage Charter

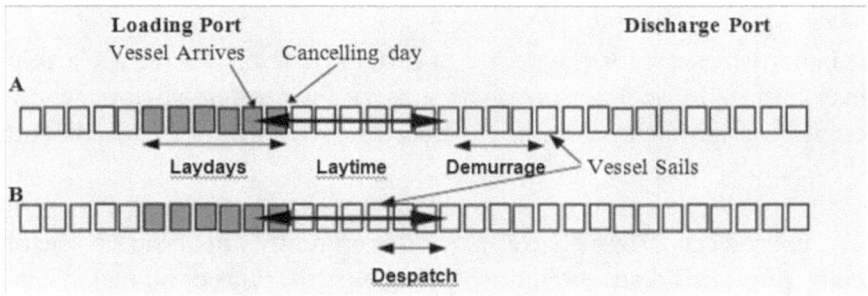

Different Types of Charter Parties

Time Charter Party

In this case, the company's need for a ship may be of a relatively short duration, and going to the expense and trouble of buying a ship or leasing a ship and having the complications of hiring and controlling a crew may not be economically viable.

In this form of charter, the charterer will hire the vessel for a prescribed period during which he will operate it as his own ship; a common reason for time charter parties is as temporary replacement for one of the companies own indisposed vessels.

A time charter party is a contract where the shipowner offers his ship and crew for hire. The vessel generally going wherever the charterer directs.

The contract is for a period of time during which the charterer is to have the right within agreed limits of directing how the ship shall be used and is to pay for her in proportion to the time used. The hire payable strictly on the dates agreed in the charter; otherwise the shipowner may have the right to withdraw his vessel or not.

During the period of the charter, the charterer will bear the cost of any delays due to shipping operations, e.g., cargo port delays, but will normally be compensated for delays due to the operation of the ship, e.g., downtime or off hire.

It is not necessary for the period of hire to be fixed; frequently a ship may be hired under a time charter party for a single voyage, whose duration might be uncertain. Here the charterer will bear the risk and the cost of any delays in the voyage.

The contract of a time charter party is commonly drawn up on one of many pro forma distributed by shipping organizations or oil major, e.g., Baltime 1939 or Shelltime.

The shipowner retains full possession of their ship and, in most cases, is fully liable for the safety of the ship and its safe operation.

A time charter party is a contract where the shipowner offers the use of his ship and crew for a limited period. The vessel generally going wherever the charterer directs. The remuneration for a time charter is called *hire* and is payable at an agreed rate per agreed time period.

The hire is payable strictly on the dates agreed in the charter; otherwise, the shipowner may have the right to withdraw his vessel (*Mardorf Peach v. Attica Sea Carriers* (1977)) or not (*The Brimnes* (1972), *The Afouos* (1983))!

In this form of charter, the charterer will hire the vessel for a prescribed period during which he will operate it as his own ship. A common reason for time charter parties is as temporary replacement for one of the companies own indisposed vessels.

During the period of the charter, the charterer will bear the cost of any delays due to shipping operations, e.g., cargo port delays, but will normally be compensated for delays due to the operation of the ship, e.g., downtime or off hire.

It is not necessary for the period of hire to be fixed; frequently a ship may be hired under a time charter party for a single voyage, whose duration might be uncertain. Here the charterer will bear the risk and the cost of any delays in the voyage.

Using a contract, such as Shelltime, means that the charterer and the shipowner are fully aware of the expressed clause included in it and of the implied provisions that courts have decided should be so obvious that they need not be included. Any other interpretations will be included in a list of Special Clauses.

Clauses of Time Charter Party

It is important that all aspects of the charter party are understood. Certain items have a higher importance.

Shipowner. He is entitled to transfer the ownership of the vessel during the period of the charter party, usually with charterer's consent.

Responsibility and exemption. "By want of due diligence," any claim against the shipowner for delay or loss, damage to goods, or loss of freight by the charterer has to be substantiated by proof that the shipowner was negligent and did not take reasonable steps to mitigate such loss or delay.

Period of hire. This is at the charterer's option and can occasionally be extended at the charterer's option.

Time of delivery. The implication that the ship will proceed forthwith or without delay to the port of loading is not a condition. If the shipowner breaks this term of the contract and the vessel delays before proceeding to the port of loading, the charterer is entitled to damages. Where the charter does expressly provide for the time when the charterers have to give directions for the available berth to which the vessel is to go to make her delivery, the necessary inference is that directions have to be given on arrival at the port or before arrival.

Present position. At the date of the charter party's making or signing the position of the ship is a condition of the charter party (*Behn v. Burness* (1863)).

Cancelling date. The fixing of a cancelling date in a charter party merely gives warning to the shipowner that non-arrival by that date may go to the root of the contract so as to entitle the charterer to rescind the agreement. It does not relieve the shipowner of his primary obligation to proceed with all convenient speed to the port of loading.

Redelivery place or range. It is important to the shipowner; he will not want the vessel delayed or in a condition that requires time-wasting repairs. The location for redelivery is usually decided with a view to subsequent charters, and a breach of such a clause entitles the shipowner to claim damages.

State on redelivery. Where damage, in excess of "fair wear and tear," has been inflicted on the ship, the owner is entitled to damages; though he cannot insist on the charterer effecting the repairs before redelivery, he can claim for loss of profit while she is being repaired.

Final voyage. A charterer will be in breach if he sends the ship on a voyage that he does not reasonably expect to finish after the stated period. If the charterer sends the vessel on her last voyage at a time when there is no expectation that she will be redelivered within a reasonable time of the end of the period of the charter party, and she is redelivered late, he is guilty of a breach of contract. Where the charter period is for a stated time, e.g., three or six months, without an expressed additional allowance, the court may imply a reasonable allowance because of the impossibility of calculating exactly when a voyage will end.

If the charterer sends the vessel on a voyage that it is reasonably expected will be completed by the end of the charter period, the shipowner must obey the directions. If she is delayed by causes for which neither party is responsible, hire is payable at the charter rate until redelivery, even though the market rate may have gone up or down.

Cancelling. The cancelling clause exists so that the charterer has the option, under the terms of the contract, to repudiate in certain circumstances. A cancelling clause is a forfeiture clause and "so not to be applied lightly." The shipowner is under a duty to send the vessel to the port of loading even though it is impossible for her to get there by the cancelling date. If he does not do so, the charterer can sue for any damage which may have resulted. Expenses incurred due to non-arrival of the vessel can be claimed by the charterer from the shipowner. There is no contractual right to rescind a charter party unless and until the date specified in the clause has been reached.

Nationality of a vessel. It is a warranty and a change in circumstances which results in the registered nationality of the ship altering, which is a breach of contract for which the charterers may obtain damages.

Class. It is a condition at the time of making the charter, a breach of which entitles the charterer to treat the contract as discharged. The loss of class during the period of the charter may have been caused by unseaworthiness, or some other breach of the shipowner's obligation, for which the charterer would have a remedy.

Bunker fuel. One used by the vessel must comply with the owner's requirements, subject to costs being borne by the owner for more expensive grades. If the price of bunkers is not mentioned, it is implied that both parties must pay a reasonable price, i.e., the market price.

Permanent bunkers. All ships carry a minimum amount in bunkers as a safety precaution; this small quantity of oil will be carried on board at all times and will thus reduce the cargo carrying capacity of the vessel.

Bunkers on redelivery. This enables the shipowner to keep within the prescribed safety limits with regard to bunkers on board at all times.

Gross/net tonnage. The volume of the total under deck space and the volume of the cargo carrying capacity. Capacity for a particular cargo and registered tonnage are conditions of the contract where the charterer has undertaken to load a full cargo. Otherwise, it is not and may not even amount to a warranty if it is irrelevant.

Speed. Capability in knots and the consumption of fuel. A statement in the charter party of the ship's speed amounts only to a promise that the ship, at the time of making the charter, is capable of the stated speed and not that she will continue to be capable of it throughout the charter party.

Condition of vessel. There is in time charters an implied undertaking of seaworthiness at the beginning of the time of the period of hire. Unseaworthiness by itself does not entitle the charterer to repudiate the contract. He can only do so if the delay in putting the defects right is such as to amount to a frustration of the charter party.

Cargo exclusion. This disallows the charterer from carrying all types of commodities, though it will normally exclude only dangerous and noxious substances. The charterers must provide for shipment, cargo in the condition and of the kind usually shipped at the port in question or cargo of a kind described in the charter party. If the charter party merely describes the cargo to be carried as "lawful merchandise," the charterers must provide cargo which may be lawfully shipped from the port of loading and lawfully carried to and discharged at the port ordered by the charterers.

Trade limits. This can be specified in a time charter, and when they are, there must be a clear definition as to the area covered. The charter party may state that the charterer has the privilege of breaching the trading limits by paying an extra insurance premium.

Load/discharge. All ports attended during the charter are to be good and safe, where the vessel can "safely lie always afloat" (unless otherwise provided in the charter party). This phrase is concerned with the marine characteristics of the place and is not to be confused with a "safe port."

Safe port. A port will not be safe unless, in the relevant period of time, the particular ship can reach it, use it, and return from it without, in the absence of some abnormal occurrence, being exposed to damage, which cannot be avoided by good navigation and seamanship.

Charter hire. It is normally agreed on a contractual basis, where no sum has been agreed, the hire must be equitable, or sometimes the rate is calculated according to a standard scale like the International Tanker Nominal Freight Scale. A charterer may set off certain claims against hire, even where the contract does not expressly give him the right to do so. If the shipowner wrongly and in breach of contract deprives the charterer for a time of the use of the vessel, the charterer can deduct a sum equivalent to the hire for the time so lost.

Hire. It is only interrupted by the occurrence of some event that takes the ship off hire under a charter clause or the contract is frustrated.

Hire payment. The charterer is liable to pay hire in advance. The charter party will state the currency to be used in accounting, e.g., sterling or US dollars.

Off-hire clause. Since it operates for the benefit of the charterer, it will be construed in favor of the shipowner if it's meaning is not clear. The clause provides that in the event of time being lost in circumstances that prevent the working of the vessel for more than twenty-four hours, payment of hire shall cease until she is again efficient to resume service. If the time lost exceeds twenty-four hours, hire is not payable in respect of the first twenty-four hours. If a vessel breaks down and puts into a port for repairs, she is off hire, but hire will be payable again when she is fit to sail again from that place and not from the time she reaches the location of her breakdown. Hire recommences as soon as the ship is able to resume service though she is not then in the same geographical position and though in effect the charterer has to pay twice for the same part of the voyage.

Place of arbitration. In most charter parties, it is effected through London or New York, with organizations like the London Maritime Arbitrators Association (LMAA) or law courts like the Commercial Division of the High Court of Justice.

Lien. The right to hold property until a debt is paid off.

Salvage. The act of, and the money paid for, saving property of a ship and/or cargo; it is a contractual agreement, and in time charters, the award is normally paid equally to the shipowner and the charterer.

Additional clauses. The additional clauses are agreed by the parties to the contract and are normally appended as typewritten sheets to the signed charter party.

Voyage Charter Party

i. Contract for the use of the ship, on a voyage or series of voyages, in carrying goods to be shipped by the charterer, or in his name. The charterer agreeing to pay for the ship either in proportion to the goods carried or a lump sum for the voyage or in proportion to the time occupied.
ii. Contracts similar to it, but by which liberty is given to the charterer to use the ship for the purpose of taking goods of other shippers and to require the master to give bills of lading for goods so shipped.

A company needs a ship for a very limited period to carry a one-off large amount of cargo between two specific areas. In this case, their need is satisfied by a voyage charter from a port of loading to a port of discharge.

The shipowner retains full control and has full liability for his ship.

The voyage charter party is a contract to carry specified goods on a defined voyage between two named ports. The remuneration of the shipowner from a voyage charter party is *freight*, calculated according to the quantity of cargo loaded or carried or sometimes a lump sum freight for the complete voyage.

In the tanker trade, *freight* is usually calculated on Worldscale.

To assist the shipowner in maximizing the benefit of the voyage, all voyage charter parties have certain attributes that are based on the need to

- Reduce time delays that are a result of the action or inaction of the charterer
- Charterer not being ready for the ship
- Loading/discharge difficulties or delays
- Tardiness in releasing a loaded ship
- Provide a secure place to load or discharge the ship
- To provide the agreed amount of cargo

Reducing Time Delays

The most obvious way of ensuring that time delays are kept to a minimum is to put a financial obligation on the charterer for avoidable idleness on his part. This must not be viewed as a penalty, more as "liquidated damages" (*Hardley v. Baxendale* (1854)).

So that both parties to the contract know what is expected of them regarding the duration of the voyage, the voyage charter party will include detail provisions for the following:

- How much time is to be spent loading and unloading,
- When the agreed time should begin to count,
- Who has responsibility for what delay,
- The amount of money due to the shipowner for delay or the bonus payable to the charterer for finishing before the allotted time.

Variations of voyage charter parties can include the following:

- *Gross form*, where the shipowner pays all the cargo costs
- *Free in and out*, where the charterer pays loading and discharging expenses
- *Port, dock, and berth charters* determine the commencement of lay time and where the vessel can be considered an arrived ship.

Some forms of general charter parties are adaptable enough to encompass these variations though others are specific charters for a specified trade.

Some commonly used voyage charter parties include Gen Con for dry cargo, Shellvoy 5, and Asbatankvoy.

A specific charter would be one like the North American Grain Charter Party 1973 (NORGRAIN), which covers the carriage of grain and includes special clauses on self-trimming bulk carriers (Cl.12) and St. Lawrence Seaway Tolls (Cl. 26).

The fundamental aspect of a voyage charter party is that since the freight payable is not dependent on the duration of the voyage but on the amount of cargo carried, it is the shipowner not the charterer that bears the cost of any delays, and it is incumbent on the charterer to provide the agreed amount of cargo.

Clauses of a Voyage Charter Party

Deadweight cargo. This is a guarantee of the carrying capacity of the ship, without reference to any particular cargo proposed to be shipped, where reference to a particular cargo is made the guarantee will relate to the capacity to carry that cargo. If the vessel is chartered for a lump sum freight but is incapable of carrying the guaranteed capacity the charterer will be entitled to damages.

Now in position. It is a stipulation as to the position of the ship and is a condition of the contract, noncompliance of which means the charterer is entitled to treat the contract as repudiated and refuse to load.

Expected ready to load. This express provision, that the ship will be ready to load, is a condition. A breach of which allows the charterer to refuse to load. He is also entitled to damages unless the breach was caused by an excepted peril or if the venture has been frustrated.

Notice of Readiness

A notice of readiness (NOR) is a communication to the charterer, shipper, receiver, or other persons, as required by the charter, that the ship has arrived at the port or berth, as the case may be, and is ready to load/discharge (Charterparty Definitions (1980)).

The NOR must be given in accordance with the procedure in the notice clause or lay time clause in the C/P. The NOR must be given within the "lay can" period and before lay time can commence. The NOR usually is tendered during office hours from Monday to Saturday (but check the C/P for instructions). The C/P will normally state that lay time will commence a certain number of hours after NOR is given or accepted.

If this is not stated, lay time will commence as soon as NOR is given. A few minutes delay in tendering on a Saturday morning could mean that lay time will not commence until Tuesday morning, even though cargo work starts earlier.

The NOR usually need only be tendered at the first of two or more load ports, unless the C/P provides otherwise. Most modern charter parties contain an expressed provision making a written notice of readiness obligatory at all ports of loading and discharging.

The NOR may (in common law) be oral, but for practical purposes (and because nearly all C/Ps require it) should be given in writing. The NOR may be tendered by delivery of a printed form or letter or by telex, fax, or cable, unless the C/P provides otherwise.

The NOR must be addressed to charterers or their agent, *not* the owner's agent.

"Arrived ship"

To determine whether the vessel has become an "arrived ship" within the C/P terms, the master will need to know whether the C/P is a "port C/P" or a "berth C/P." Which party bears the risk of delay following arrival of the vessel will depend on which type the C/P is. The agreed voyage is defined by the places named in the C/P for loading and discharging. If a port is defined as the place for loading, without stipulating a particular berth, the C/P is a port C/P. In this case, the vessel becomes an arrived ship when

- She has entered port limits,
- Is fully at the charterer's disposal, and
- Is fully ready to load in a place where ships waiting for berth in the port usually wait.

It is not necessary for the vessel to be on her loading berth to be an "arrived ship" under a port C/P. All delays in berthing will be for the charterers' account, and this is the more favorable C/P for owners. (Asbatankvoy, Exxonvoy, and Beepeevoy are examples of port C/P).

If a particular berth is defined as the loading place, the C/P is a berth C/P. In this case, the vessel becomes an arrived ship only when she arrived at the named berth. (Shellvoy 3, 4, and 5 are examples of berth C/Ps).

To protect themselves, owners will often

- Insert a "Waiting for Berth" clause; or
- Insert the words "whether in berth or not," "whether in port or not," or some other protecting phrase in the lay time clause to make it clear that time can count as lay time once the vessel is at the customary waiting place.

Sometimes doubt arises as to whether the ship is at the place where notice should be given. In such a case, it would seem prudent to follow the advice given by the judge in the Timna case:

"I have considerable sympathy with the master in his predicament. It is a good working rule in such situations to give notice of readiness and to go on giving notices in order that when later lawyers are brought in, no one shall be able to say "if only the master had given notice of readiness, lay time would have begun and the owners would now be able to claim demurrage" (*The Timna* (1970)).

It would, therefore, be sensible, whenever in doubt, to serve notice of readiness on the charterers.

If the charterer does not have notice and is not otherwise aware of the readiness of the ship to load or discharge, lay time may not begin.

When in doubt about notice of readiness, *ask*!

"The ship is in all respects ready to load" means the vessel is seaworthy and in every way fit to carry the particular cargo on the voyage contemplated by the charterer. The vessel must be fully at the charterer's disposal, i.e., with derricks or cranes ready for operation; holds or tanks cleaned, prepared and surveyed; free pratique and customs clearance granted,

etc.—unless the C/P allows otherwise, which it may do by the inclusion of a protecting phrase.

At common law, the duty to provide a seaworthy ship on presentation was absolute, i.e., no exceptions were allowed. However, most modern C/P forms have reduced the absolute obligation to a duty of exercising "due diligence," i.e., doing everything that a prudent shipowner can reasonably do to make the vessel seaworthy without actually guaranteeing her seaworthiness.

Lay days. The period at the beginning of a charter party during which the vessel must arrive at the location of loading. The last day of "lay days" is the cancelling day.

Cancelling date. The fixing of a cancelling date in the charter party merely gives warning to the shipowner that non-arrival by the cancelling date may go to the root of the contract so as to rescind. It does not relieve the shipowner of his primary obligation to proceed with all convenient speed to the port of loading, or of his secondary obligation, in the event of nonperformance, to make reparation in money to the charterer for any loss sustained by him as a result of such nonperformance.

Port. An area within which ships are loaded with and/or discharged of cargo and includes the usual places where ships wait for their turn or are ordered or obliged to wait for their turn no matter the distance from that area (BIMCO Charterparty Definitions (1980)).

"As she may safely get." Where the charter expressly provides that a ship shall go to a safe port nominated by the charterer; he warrants that the port is safe. Also it must be a port from which she can safely depart. If it is not safe, the ship can refuse to obey the order, e.g., insufficient water.

Safe port. A port which, during the relevant period of time, the ship can reach, enter, remain at, and depart from without, in the absence of some abnormal occurrence, being exposed to danger, which cannot be avoided by good navigation and seamanship (BIMCO Charterparty Definitions).

A temporary condition of danger will not make the port unsafe, provided that such condition will not last an unreasonable time. If the charterer nominates an unsafe port and the ship is damaged through going there, he will be liable for the damage, subject to the negligence of the master; i.e., the master knew the port was unsafe but insisted on going there. If the captain acted reasonably, the charterer is liable.

Near. This is to relieve the shipowner of an absolute obligation to enter the port named in spite of sandbars, ice, or blockade. The clause only relates to obstacles that are regarded as permanent or which would require the ship to wait more than a reasonable time before adopting an alternative place, unless the cause might be regarded as a "contemplated incident of the voyage" (*Metcalfe v. Brittania Ironworks Co.* (1877), where a vessel spent five months off the frozen Sea of Azof). The distance "near" is based on commercial knowledge and experience (*The Athamas* (1963), where the distance was 250 miles in a different country).

"Safely as a laden ship." The ship is not bound to load part of the cargo in port and then take on board outside the port the part of the cargo she could not safely load in the port, unless this practice is a custom of the port.

If the ship is to load in a tidal harbor or river with a bar and her loading is being completed at neap tides, the captain is not entitled to sail with less than a full cargo, though that is all with which, at the then state of the tides, he can get out. He must complete his cargo and wait for the spring tide that will enable him to leave.

Always afloat. It is concerned exclusively with the marine characteristics of the port and requires that the vessel shall at all times be waterborne. It will not justify a vessel in declining to go to a berth where she cannot lie continuously always afloat if she can do so partly before and after neap tides.

Vessel shall proceed. In the absence of express stipulations to the contrary, the owner of a vessel implicitly undertakes to proceed in that ship by a usual and reasonable route and without unreasonable delay. The route is normally the direct geographical route, but other routes are permissible where it can be proved in that case. A route may be a "usual and reasonable" although only followed by ships of a particular line and recently adopted. It is justifiable to deviate in order to save life or to communicate with a ship in distress or if it is involuntary, e.g., as a result of necessity. In the absence of an express clause, it is not justifiable if only to save property of others.

Deviation clause. This clause allows the shipowner to proceed on a course other than "usual and reasonable" to save property.

Reaching the agreed destination stated in the charter party may be an area such as a river or port or a precise place such as a particular berth, wharf, dock, or mooring. An area may be stated with a proviso that, on arrival there, the ship is to proceed to a particular port nominated by the charterer at a later date.

The three main categories of stated destinations are those included in the following charter parties:

- *Berth charter.* When a berth or wharf is named as destination, or is to be named later, the ship reaches the agreed destination on berthing alongside. Even where there is congestion in the port, bad weather, or unfavorable tides, etc., any risk of delay in going alongside falls on the shipowner, for lay time will not start to count until the ship is alongside the berth nominated by the charter party.
- *Dock charter.* When the charter party names a dock as the destination or provides for a dock to be named later, the ship becomes an arrived ship on entering the dock. The same principle applies if a quay or roadstead is named.
- *Port charter.* When a port is named, the ship has reached the agreed destination when she has reached the place, within the commercial area of the port, where ships proposing to load or discharge her type of cargo usually wait, at the disposal of the charterers.

This position may be modified by using an expressed term such as *"Ship to proceed to . . . Or as near thereto as she may safely get."* This gives the shipowner an alternative contractual destination when an obstruction, which cannot be overcome by any reasonable means, makes it impossible to reach the agreed named destination, without waiting an unreasonable time. By reaching the alternative destination, the ship becomes an arrived ship for the purpose of satisfying the provisions of the lay time clause. Ice, blockades, congestion, tides, etc., could prevent the ship reaching the agreed destination, and with the above wording in the charter party, lay time would count as soon as the ship reached an alternative destination allowed by the phrase *"as near thereto as she may safely get."*

Cargo

Description must be one reasonably complying with the terms of the charter.

Full and complete cargo according to the custom of the port of loading. The charterer is under an obligation and is entitled to load the full cargo. Where the charter party authorizes the loading of several types of cargo, the charterer may load a full cargo of any one, or more of them, even though this does not provide as much freight as expected; however, he cannot choose to load goods that leave excessive broken stowage. He is obliged to fill up the spaces.

The obligation to load is absolute, and he is excused only where his failure to load is due to the fault of the shipowner or where it is covered by an express provision of the charter party or where the charter party is frustrated. The charterer cannot limit his obligation to the capacity named in the charter party, but he must load as much cargo as the ship will carry with safety.

Where the charterer fails to load a full and complete cargo, the shipowner may fill up with other cargo in order to minimize the damages he may claim and may delay for a reasonable time in so doing. The charterer is entitled to keep the ship in port during the lay time for as long as a full and complete cargo is not loaded, even if the cargo is deliberately withheld by the charterer.

The charterer must make and carry out arrangements for delivery of the cargo at the ship's side at the place of loading in time to load her within the agreed time after arrival and in ordinary circumstances nothing which prevents him from doing so will relieve him from his express or implied obligations to load in a fixed or reasonable time.

In the absence of express provisions, the charterer will not be relieved from this obligation by causes preventing a cargo from being obtained such as follows:

- Strikes (*Grant v. Coverdale* (1884))
- Bankruptcy of merchants supplying cargo (*Stephens v. Harris* (1887))
- Nonexistence of cargo (*Hills v. Sughrue* (1846))

or by causes preventing a cargo, when obtained, from being transmitted to the port of loading such as follows:

- Ice (*Grant v. Coverdale* (1884))
- Bad weather (*Fenwick v. Schmalz* (1868))
- Railway delays (*Adams v. Royal Mail Steam Co.* (1858))
- Government orders (*Ford v. Cotesworth* (1868)).

The charterer must perform his part of the operation of putting cargo on board, unless excused by express exceptions, the causes excepted being proved not merely to exist but also directly involved in preventing the vessel being loaded. If the charterer proves that the usual and proper method of loading was prevented by excepted peril, the onus shifts to the shipowner to prove the existence of an alternative method.

Freight

Freight is the remuneration payable by charterers to owners for the performance of the contracts and may be called *charter party freight.*

Freight must be paid, under common law, on delivery of the cargo to the consignee or his receiver at the agreed destination, in the absence of any term to the contrary.

Freight is normally payable in accordance with the terms of a freight clause, which stipulates the amount of freight, the time for payment, and the method of payment.

Freight is often payable under the C/P terms partially in advance, e.g., on loading or on the issue of B/L.

Freight may depend in amount on the in-taken weight of cargo, the outturn weight, the cargo volume, cargo value, or on some other stipulated basis.

Freight is not payable unless the entire cargo reaches the agreed destination, even if not the carrier's fault, e.g., if the voyage is abandoned after a general average act. (Owners usually protect themselves by insuring against possible loss of freight so that the freight insurers become a party to the "common adventure" in general average cases).

Freight is not payable where owners have breached the contract, but when cargo is delivered damaged, full freight is normally payable, and a separate claim is presented by the cargo owners for damage.

If freight is payable in advance, it is collected by the port agent at the loading port before issue of a "freight paid" bill of lading.

If freight is payable on discharge, it is collected by the port agent on presentation of an original bill of lading by the receiver.

Freight is not payable on delivery if cargo has lost its "specie," i.e., changed its physical nature.

Freight may be of the following kinds:

- Charter party freight (described above)
- Lump sum freight

- Bill of lading freight
- Advance or prepaid freight
- Pro rata freight
- Ad valorem freight
- Back freight or
- Dead freight

Lump sum freight is not calculated on cargo carried but on the voyage. To earn lump sum freight, either the ship must complete the voyage or the cargo must be transshipped and delivered by the shipowner to its destination.

Bill of lading freight is freight calculated on shipped or in-taken weights as stated in a B/L and may be payable in advance or at destination.

Advance freight is deemed to be earned as the cargo is loaded and may be the total freight or an agreed proportion of it, payable in advance at the loading port, the balance being payable on delivery of the cargo. It is not refundable if the vessel and cargo is lost. This type of freight is commonly required where cargo is shipped under a transferable B/L as buyers of goods covered by a B/L often require a "freight paid" B/L. It is also often demanded by carriers of dry cargoes and is usual in the liner trade.

Pro rata freight is payable in common law where only part of the voyage has been completed, e.g., when the voyage is abandoned following an outbreak of war or an accident and cargo is discharged at an intermediate port or if the vessel had to leave port because of onset of ice.

Ad valorem freight is freight charged as a percentage of the value of a shipment, usually of high-value goods, and is not normally used in voyage C/Ps, generally being confined to liner shipments. An ad valorem B/L is one on which the value of the cargo is recorded and under which the owner waives his right to limit his liability to the goods owner under the package limitation provisions in the contract, usually in return for the higher ad valorem freight.

Back freight. Normal delivery at the port of destination may sometimes be prevented by some cause beyond the control of the master, e.g., a failure on the part of the cargo owner to take delivery. In such a case, the master may and must deal with the cargo for the benefit of its owner by landing it, carrying it on, or transshipping it, as may seem best. The shipowner may then charge the cargo owner to cover the expenses thus incurred for his actions and efforts.

Dead freight is the name given to the damages to which a shipowner is entitled for the charterer's breach of the contract in failing to load a full cargo. To sustain such a claim, the shipowner must prove that the charterer or shipper was aware that the vessel could carry more cargo and was given reasonable opportunity to provide the balance before the vessel left the loading port. If the charterer fails to supply a complete cargo, the shipowner is not only permitted to take reasonable steps to fill the ship with other cargo but he may also be obliged to do so in mitigation of his damages for dead freight. The shipowner is not entitled to dead freight because, by the method chosen, less cargo can be loaded than by another usual method.

Where the ship takes on board all she can ship, though in fact she loads less than a full cargo, the full facts have to be considered before arriving at a conclusion as to whether or not the charterer is liable for dead freight.

Freight payable. When there is no provision to the contrary, freight is payable on the delivery of the goods.

Loading/Discharging Costs

Gross terms. The shipowner pays all the major costs of loading and discharging. The charterer has only the cost of delivery to the ship and the cost of heavy lifts loaded into the ship.

FIO (free in/out). The charterer pays the total loading and discharging expenses.

Lay Time

Lay time is the time allowed to charterers for cargo operations.

Lay time is defined as *the period of time agreed between the parties during which the owner will make and keep the ship available for loading/discharging without payment additional to the freight.*

Lay time should, in the interests of owners, start as soon as practicable.

Lay time may be *separate* for load and discharge ports, or *reversible* (or '*all purposes*'); the master should check the C/P.

Lay time may be of three types:

- *Definite lay time* is stated in the C/P as a definite period of time, e.g., "6 (six) days . . ." or "48 running hours."
- *Calculable lay time* is determined by making a calculation from information in the C/P, e.g., Where a cargo weighing 20,000 tons is to be loaded at a rate of 10,000 tons per day, the lay time is 2 days.
- *Indefinite lay time* the C/P may state that the cargo is to be loaded with *"customary dispatch"* or *"customary quick dispatch"* or *"as fast as the vessel can receive."*

Lay time cannot start to count against charterers until three conditions are fulfilled:

- The vessel has become an "arrived ship" within the terms of the C/P
- The vessel is in all respects ready to load/discharge, and
- Notice of readiness has been served on charterers or their agent (or, in few cases, such as under the Shellvoy 4 C/P, when NOR has been *received* by charterers or their agent.

Owner's Responsibility

The shipowner is quite free to exclude his liability for loss or damage to cargo in any way that he thinks fit with an express clause. In most charter parties, the owner is responsible for loss or damage to goods only where the loss has been caused by the management of the cargo or "personal want of due diligence" to make the ship seaworthy.

The owner is not responsible for loss by any other cause, even neglect or from unseaworthiness of the vessel on loading or commencement of the voyage or at any time.

Other Clauses
- *Clause paramount.* It identifies the wording of a clause to be inserted in the bill of lading, the authority of the Hague Rules or the Hague-Visby Rules or Hamburg Rules.
- *Lien clause.* Lien is the name given to the shipowner's right to retain possession of the goods carried on board his ship as security for payment of freight and other charges.
- *Cancelling clause.* It may exist in a charter party so that the charterer has the option, under the terms of the contract, of repudiating in certain circumstances.
- *General average.* Money paid out by all involved in the contract for losses that arise in consequence of extraordinary sacrifices made or expenses incurred for the preservation of the ship and/or cargo. The amounts due are proportional to the interest that the participants had in the venture.
- *Indemnity.* The shipowner maybe entitled, either by implication of law or by express agreement, to be recompensed by the charterer for loss caused by the charterer's actions. This recompense in monetary terms is based on the total freight due.
- *General strike clause.* This clause is needed to explain the limits of the charterer's liability with regard to strikes. This exception only covers stoppages arising out of trade disputes.

Importance of Time and Cargo

When the shipowner and charterer have agreed on the freight rate to be paid, it becomes of paramount importance that the conditions in the charter party regarding the times allowed for loading/discharging and the amount of cargo to be loaded are strictly adhered to; otherwise, the shipowner's calculation will count for nothing, and he would not be operating at an economic rate.

To increase the charterer's awareness of the importance of time and cargo, there are clauses included in the charter party that state he agrees to pay (liquidated damages, not penalties!) for any infringement.

Demurrage. The cost per day of any extension of time above that agreed (lay time) for loading and discharging.

Dead freight. The cost applied to any shortage of cargo below the agreed figure.

Dispatch. A repayment to shipper/charterer for releasing the ship quicker than contracted.

This is of an essence to the shipowner; he will want his ship loaded, discharged, and off the charter as soon as possible and then on to the next one.

Mechanical breakdowns and logistical and navigational problems are to his account; therefore, he has to keep a keen eye on any delays, trying to deduct them from the lay time in port or hustling the ship to make up any lost time at sea.

This is where the commercial aspects of ship operations could impinge on the safety consciousness of the shipboard teams.

Commencement of Lay Time

It is the general rule that a vessel must be an "arrived ship" before lay time can begin to count. A voyage charter party will normally provide for the beginning of lay time by the inclusion of an expressed clause stating when and how it should start.

Whether or not such a clause is contained in a charter party, the following requirements must be satisfied before lay time can begin to count:

- The ship must have reached the agreed destination.
- The ship must be ready to load or discharge.
- Notice of readiness must be given, after arrival, to the charterers or their agents.

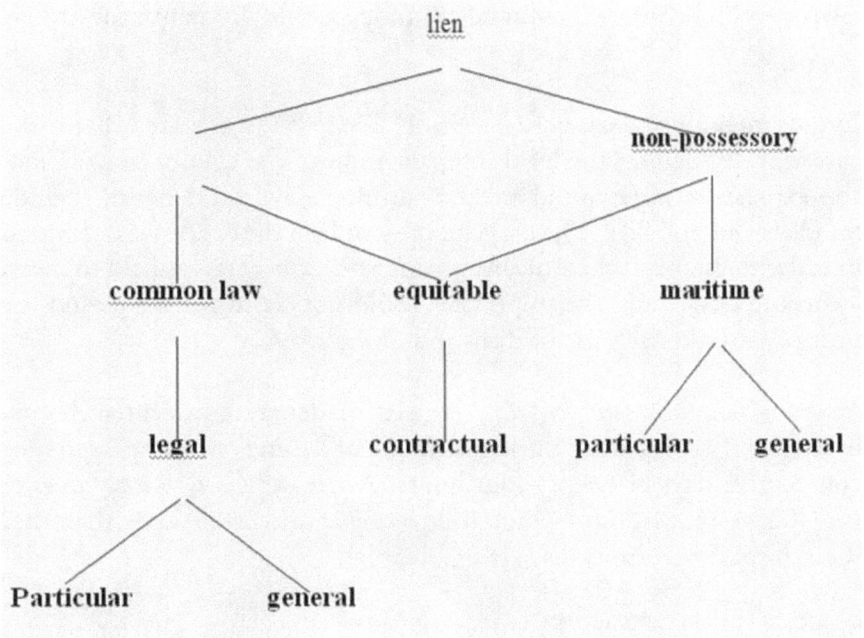

Responsibilities for Delays during Lay Time

If disputes are to be avoided, the charter party should indicate clearly the types of contingencies that are allowed to be written off as non-lay time. The most obvious problem will be over the definition of time.

Lay time clauses use various expressions such as follows:

- Day
- Weather working day
- Running day

In general, the expression *day*, without further qualification, means continuous days, e.g., Thursday to Tuesday would count as five days lay time (*not lay days*) on the basis of continuous days.

Where there is an established custom of the port not to work Sundays, lay time will be interrupted, and a Sunday would not count toward lay time.

In judgment on the case of *Cochran v. Retburg*, it was stated that if the case was decided on the legal interpretation of the clauses in isolation, the expression *days* would mean "running days" and hence include Sundays and holidays. The usage of the words in the clause was admitted in order to establish their meaning, and the term *days* was held to mean "working days," and the shipowner could not claim for the period the port's customhouse was off duty and on holiday.

Running hours or *running days* is used to denote consecutive hours, by day and night, both during and out of normal working hours, or consecutive days of twenty-four hours (*Nielsen & Co v. Wait, James & Co* (1885)), that is, days which follow one immediately after the other (Charterparty Definitions (1980)).

Sundays and Holidays Excepted (S&HE). Generally charter parties provide that these days do not count toward lay time, and the effect is that even if work is done on these days by arrangement, they do not count (*Nelson v. Nelson* (1908)). Except where there is an express condition that they do count.

After lay time has begun, there may be bad weather that interrupts or prevents work, and the effect of bad weather then depends on the wording of the lay time clause, which may refer to the following:

- Weather working days
- Weather permitting

Weather permitting or *weather working day* is a working day that is not unavailable to work because of weather, that is, a day on which the weather permits the relevant work to be done; where the weather does prevent work from being carried out, that time does not count toward lay time. The calculation of lay time must take into account the type of lay time clause that applies to decide whether a day should count as a complete day for lay time or whether the part of the twenty-four hours that has been affected by the weather should be omitted from the total.

Questions over the responsibilities of each party to the contract over delays must be found in the charter party. Clauses included in the text will give reference to specific instances of liability:

- Loading holdups due to machinery breakdowns could be for the ship's account (and not count toward lay time) if it is the fault of the ship's gear. Or it could count as lay time if the charterer is providing the equipment.
- Strikes in a port can be excluded from lay time calculations, whereas, strikes only affecting the ship in question could be included in the total lay time.

Demurrage

When the agreed time for loading or discharging, with allowances for weather, holidays, etc., has been used, the shipowner should be able to sail or, if discharging, is due his ship back for further employment. However, this will not always be possible because it is probable that the cargo has not all been loaded or, at the discharge port, there may still be cargo in its hatches waiting for off-loading.

Therefore, the shipowner should be able to obtain payment for the delay of his vessel, and conversely, the charterer should be rewarded for returning the vessel to the owner before the prescribed period has ended.

The agreed additional payments for the delay are called *demurrage*, and they are paid by the charterer to the shipowner on a day rate basis, with pro rata payment for parts of the day.

It is the money payable to the owner for delay, for which the owner is not responsible, in loading and/or discharging after the lay time has expired.

A very important point regarding demurrage is that when a charterer has used the lay time due for loading/discharging, all time counts from then on toward the damages, with no exceptions as to weather, Sundays, holidays, or whatever.

Dispatch

Dispatch is the money payable by the owner of the ship to the charterer if the ship completes loading or discharging before the lay time has expired.
This bonus payment is for *not* using all the allotted lay time. It is paid by the shipowner to the charterer as per the rates included in the charter party.

Dispatch can be paid for either

- All time saved (the time saved to the ship from completion of loading/discharging to the expiring of the lay time including periods excepted from lay time).
- All lay time saved (the time saved to the ship from completion of loading/discharging to the expiring of the lay time excluding any notice time and periods excepted from lay time).

In the absence of an expressed clause in the charter party, e.g., "Ten running days on demurrage . . . will be allowed," demurrage will be paid for a reasonable time, and the charterer may not detain the vessel indefinitely as the shipowner will be entitled to rescind the contract.

Lay Time Question

Charter party states:

- "Cargo shall be loaded at 500 tonnes per hatch per day, weather permitting, Sundays and holidays excepted."
- "Lay time shall commence at 1:00 p.m. if notice of readiness is given before noon, and at 6:00 a.m. next working day if notice given during normal office hours after noon."

- "Demurrage shall be paid at $500 per day and pro rata for any part of a day, dispatch at half demurrage for all time saved." Normal office hours are from 0900 to 1700 hrs.

Statement of Facts

Wednesday, 3rd.	1100	Vessel arrived in port.
	2000	Notice of readiness tendered and accepted.
Thursday, 4th.	0700	Work commenced in all 4 hatches to load 14,000 tonnes of cargo.
Monday, 8th.		Public holiday.
Thursday, 11th.	0900–1600	Rain stopped loading.
Tuesday, 16th.	2200	Loading completed.

Using the information supplied, calculate the amount of demurrage or dispatch due and to whom it is payable.

Lay Time Answer

Lay time 14,000 = 14,000 = 7 days
500 × 4 = 2,000

Date day	Time	Remark	Lay time	Day	Hours
Wed 3rd	1100hrs	NOR tendered	---	-----	----
Wed 3rd	2000hrs	NOR accepted	9 hours	-----	9 hours
Thu 4th	0700hrs	Commence discharge	------	------	-------
Fri 5th	------	No work	-------	1	11hrs
Sat 6th	------	No work	-------	1	11hrs
Sun 7th	Expected	Expected	Expected	Expected	Expected
Mon 8th	Holiday	Holiday	Holiday	Holiday	Holiday
Tue 9th	--------	No work	---------	1	11hrs
Wed 10th	--------	No work	---------	1	11hrs
Thu 11th	0700hrs	Rain Stop 0900-1600hr	7hours	------	7 hours
Fri 12th	0700hrs	Commence loading	--------	--------	-------
Sat 13th	0700hrs	Loading	--------	-------	---------
Sun 14th	---------	No work	--------	1	11hours
Mon 15th	----------	No work	--------	1	11hours
Tue 16th	0700hrs	2200hrs completed	----------	-------	---------

Total number of lay time = 82 hours/24 = 3 days +10 hours

Demurrage per day is tag at $ 500

500 X 3 Days = 1,500 USD

500 / 24 X 10 = 208.33 USD

Total demurrage payable by the charterer to the ship owners is $ 1708.33

Safe Port

"A port which, during the relevant period of time, the ship can reach, enter, remain at, and depart from without, in the absence of some abnormal occurrence, being exposed to danger which cannot be avoided by good navigation and seamanship" (BIMCO Charterparty Definitions (1980)).

The port is not safe, in the absence of any express agreement to the contrary, unless the ship can enter it as a laden ship carrying the cargo, which is to be delivered to the consignee there.

A port may be rendered unsafe from political matters, such as war and blockade, as well as from natural dangers of the sea, vessels sinking in fairways, and authorities closing the port due to congestion, as long as the prohibition is not merely temporary.

The charterer's obligation to nominate a safe port usually arises under an express clause in the charter party.

The vessel to be employed only between good and safe ports or places where she can safely lie (Baltime 1939, clause 2).

Many voyage charters lack such an express clause in their printed versions, e.g., Gen Con, Polcoalvoy, and a few more contain a diluted form of safe port obligation, which stipulates only that the charterer shall use due diligence to provide a safe port, e.g., Shellvoy 2 and Shelltime 3.

There is, however, an implied condition in a charter party that the charterer will name a safe port.

If a charterer names an unsafe port, the shipowner is not entitled to repudiate the charter party but must proceed to the nearest safe port and discharge the goods there.

If the charterer names an unsafe port, he will be liable to the shipowner for any damages caused to the ship by sailing there, unless the master ought to have been aware of the danger in the port named and exercised his right of proceeding to the nearest safe port.

The normal definition of safe port is derived from "a port will not be safe unless, in the relevant period of time, the particular ship can reach it, use it and return from it without, in the absence of some abnormal occurrence, being exposed to danger which cannot be avoided by good navigation and seamanship."

The doctrines of a safe port apply equally as well to a safe berth and the requirements for a time charterer to provide "good and safe ports" carries with it the obligation to nominate safe berths within such ports.

The relevant period of time... The contractual promise is that the port will be safe when the ship has to use it. If, unknown to anyone, access to the port is, in fact, blocked by a submerged wreck at the time the order is given, the port will not be prospectively safe, and if damages result, the charterers will be liable.

By way of contrast, if the hidden obstruction occurs after the order is given but before the ship arrives, the time charterer is obliged to do all he can to protect the ship from the new danger. This secondary obligation does not arise if the charterer has no means of knowing about the new "unexpected and abnormal occurance."
Thus, it is for shipowners, whose ships are damaged in incidents of secondary obligations, to prove that the charterers ought to have foreseen the danger presented by the intervening danger.

A temporary danger or obstruction will not render the port as unsafe if the carrier could wait a reasonable while for the obstruction to be removed and then proceed into the port.

Neap tides do not make a port unsafe.

The law does not require the port to be safe at the very time of the vessel's arrival. Just as the ship may encounter wind and weather conditions that delay her on voyage to the port, so may she be delayed by similar conditions on her arrival that put back her entry into the port, and the charterer cannot be held responsible for one delay and not the other.

A port is not necessarily unsafe just because a vessel might have to leave it on the approach of bad weather, for it to be safe though, there must be

   a. an adequate weather forecasting system
   b. adequate availability of pilots
   c. adequate sea room to maneuver
   d. an adequate system for ensuring that the sea room was always available.

A port must be safe in its "set up," which consists of the provisions of equipment, such as properly functioning navigation lights and part in services rendered by tugs, pilots, and meteorological stations, or the port must make it clear to masters that they must themselves keep a wireless watch.

The particular ship. A port can be held unsafe for a particular ship, where it might be the largest ever to call at the port and could not enter without tugs that were not available locally.

Reach it, use it, and return from it. When something occurs that stops the vessel from arriving at the port, e.g., ice.

It is immaterial in point of law where the danger is located though it is obvious that the more remote it is from the port, the less likely it is to interfere with the safety of the voyage.

The charterer does not guarantee that the most direct route to the port is safe, but the voyage he orders must be one that an ordinarily prudent and skillful master can find a way of making in safety.

If access to the port is dangerous, owing to the operation of submarines in wartime, the port may be unsafe, even though there is no danger in the port itself.

For a port to be safe, it must be one that she can safely get out of, e.g., Not be obstructed by bridges when sailing out in ballast.

In the absence of some abnormal occurrence. An event is not "abnormal" merely because it has hardly ever happened before. Rocket attacks in Beirut were not considered abnormal as they were an inherent feature of that port in 1978.

Good navigation and seamanship. If the effective cause of the damage suffered by a ship is her own poor navigation, then it follows that the safety or lack of safety of the port is beside the point.

Operating Costs

The allocation of costs is based on the following:

- Type of charter party
- Clauses of charter party

Costs in running a ship can be subdivided into two main categories:

- Operating costs, which exist if the ship is working or not
- Voyage costs, which are incurred when the vessel is actually working

Based on this, the costs involved in a charter can be allocated.

Demise or Bareboat Charter Party

The shipowner is responsible for the financing of the ship, and the demise charterer is normally responsible for all other expenses, as though he were the owner.

Time Charter Party

The shipowner's hire rate will be based on his *operating costs*. In a bad market, the hire may not cover all these expenses:

- Financing of the ship
- Hull and machinery insurance (if any)
- P & I cover, including additional pollution insurance
- Membership of required organizations
- Crew wages and expenses, such as travel, food, etc.
- Maintenance
- Lubricating oils
- Dry-docking expenses
- Statutory certification
- Classification
- Management
- Views of the current and future market. This is also related to the "lay up" or "trade" decision.

The charterer usually pays for the *voyage costs/running*:

- Fuel
- Port and harbor charges or dues
- Tugs and pilots
- Loading and discharging expenses
- Crew's overtime, if used for cargo purposes

Once the charterer has taken over the commercial operation of the ship, the shipowner is paid "hire" whether the ship is carrying cargo and working or not.

The charterer's main operational concern is that the ship

- *Performs* as well as the charter party states in speed, carrying capacity, load/discharge rates, heating/cooling of cargo, etc.
- Has a *crew* who are experienced and reliable
- *Does not experience "off-hire,"* due to some mechanical or logistical reason, for example, engine malfunction or no ship's captain, and the ship is incapable of work
- Provides effective *communication*

Some charter parties contain a clause stating a minimum period of time (example twenty-four hours) before "off hire" is activated.

Voyage Charter Party

The shipowner will pay for almost every item of voyage expense

- Operating costs
- Voyage costs

He will also have to estimate cost of mobilizing his ship, positioning cost, to the load port, and demobilizing after he has finally discharged the cargo to another loading area.

The operating cost of the time taken to load and discharge his ship must also be taken into account. In addition the voyage costs of this period must be included, i.e., port charges, pilotage, tugs, fuel, overtime, etc., used.

Once he has calculated the total cost and the likely period of time the charter will take to complete, he can arrive at a freight rate, dollar per tonne, for the specified cargo.

The charterer will often be responsible for load/discharge costs, except when the owner pays extra to ensure the vessel leaves before the end of lay time.

The charterer's concerns are usually based on the quality and quantity of cargo output.

In addition there will be interest with regard to any delay in port that could be attributed to the ship, which could extend the vessel's stay and incur demurrage.

The freight rate for tankers is normally calculated by Worldscale, where most of the port charges are allowed for.

Once he has calculated the total cost and the likely period of time the charter will take to complete, he can arrive at a freight rate, dollar per tonne, for the specified cargo.

From the following example, if a ship could charge its freight on the cargo-carrying section of the voyage alone, it would prove very much less expensive for the shipper.

A marked difference in freight for the shipper to choose between!

Example

> The Strathclyde Venture is presently at Xerbi, negotiating for a voyage charter party from AJEN to BARBI with a full cargo of 18,000 tonnes of grain, loading at 3,600 tonnes per day and discharging at 6,000 tonnes per day.
>
> The next cargo will be loaded at Yberg.
>
> The ship has a daily operating cost of $12,000 and uses 20 tonnes of fuel per day on passage (fuel at $90/tonne) (Operating Cost includes profit element), and the contract is FIO (free in and out—all loading and discharging costs, including port fees, paid by charterer).

Distance Table (in days)		
Xerbi to Ajen	4 days	
Ajen to Barbi	10 days	
Loading time	= 18,000/3,600 =	5 days
Discharging time	= 18,000/6,000 =	3 days

Total days spent 22 days

Operating cost = days × cost = 22 × 12,000 = $264,000

Voyage cost = days × oil rate × oil cost
= 16 × (20 × 90) = $28,000
Total cost = $292,000

Freight rate = Total cost/cargo capacity = 292,000/18000

= $16.2 per tonne
Cargo voyage cost

If the ship could be solely costed per cargo voyage

Loading at A	5 days
Voyage from A to B	10 days
Discharging at B	3 days
Total time	18 days

Operating cost	= 18 × 1200	= $216,000
Voyage cost	= 10 × (20 × 90)	= $18,000
Total cost	= 234,000	
Freight rate	= 234,000/18,000	= $13 per tonne

Exercise 3: Choice of Charter

Vessel is discharging in Tallin and has two charter party options:

Option 1: Voyage charter party from Poland to Mauritius with 20,500 tonnes of coal at $26 per tonne (FIOS)—total distance 10,800 miles via Cape (Suez too expensive). Lay time 2 days to load, 3 days to discharge.

Option 2: Time charter party, 40 days at $11,250 per day delivery St. Petersburg and redelivery Antwerp/Hamburg Range (AHA)

Finance cost (capital and interest): $7,000 per day
Operating costs (crew, insurance, maintenance, etc.): $4,000 per day
Fuel costs: 15 knots at 25 tonnes per day at $100 per tonne.

Which charter party provides the best return and explain what other items you would look for.

Communicate and Report

Read	Ask	Tell

Communication is vital, and it must be understood by the ship's master, officers, and crew that they must

- *Read* statutory, company, and commercial documents that are carried on board the ship
- *Ask* the ship management office, operators, superintendents, and managers for clarification or additional information
- *Tell* the ship management office, operators, superintendents, and managers of all incidents that could or have affected the ship and its operation.

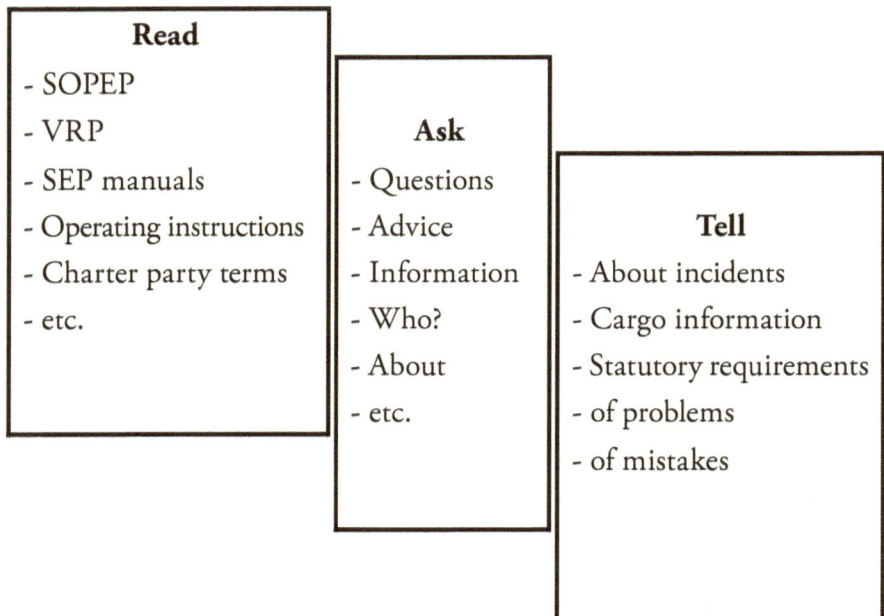

Tell: Example 1

48,000 DWT product tanker on time charter (Shelltime 4 with amendments) for about a period of one year. After many voyages carrying petroleum products, the vessel was fixed to carry a cargo of vegetable oil.

On arrival at the loading port, the ship was inspected by the shipper and the charterer's surveyor. The condition of the tanks were considered unsuitable for the carriage of vegetable oil due to severe soot staining. It was apparent that the vessel had cleaned well between cargoes as there were no traces of petroleum product in the tanks; however, it was also apparent that the incorrect operation of the inert gas plant and dirty filters had resulted in soot deposits collecting on the tank coating.

This was the first indications that the managers received that the vessel was in a condition where she could not carry cargoes according to the charter party. The master, however, told the charterers that there had been soot deposits for a considerable time, during which time he had not informed the managers.

If the master had *told the managers* about the soot deposits at an earlier date while the vessel was employed on the petroleum trade, the managers would have been able to carry out special cleaning or repair or inform the charterers and renegotiate the charter not to carry vegetable oil.

This incident resulted in a considerable cost to the owners and managers, plus longer term damage of unreliability and poor management practice.

Tell: Example 2

An oil tanker on the US Trade was boarded by the US Coast Guard at a discharge port and inspected. The authorities found three items that required attention and gave the master a list indicating that the defects must be completed before arrival in the next US port.

The master decided to ignore the list and sailed to the next load port, which was also in the United States. The vessel was again boarded by the US Coast Guard who wanted to ensure that the outstanding defects had been rectified. They had not!

The vessel was served with a detaining order and not allowed to load or sail. It was at this time that the managers heard of the problems and defects at the discharge port.

The USCG and the Paris Memorandum countries operate a common computer database that they call up when a vessel is scheduled for their area. It lists the complete history of the vessel, its incidents (if any), and defects. They are forewarned of possible defective ships.

The master should have *told the company* immediately he received the defect report, and they would have taken action to clear the problems either at the discharge port or at the load port before the coast guard had boarded.

Instead, an immense amount of time and effort was used to repair the defects *and* ensure that the ship, owners and management company were not targeted under the USCG Port State Control Initiative.

Tell: Example 3

A 96,000 DWT OBO was on a time charter and subchartered on a voyage basis to load two parcels of bulk cargo at two separate terminals.

On completion of the first parcel, a draft survey was taken by the chief officer, and the quantity of cargo calculated by himself and a surveyor. Unfortunately, an error was made in the readings of a ballast tank, which resulted in approximately 2,000 MT less cargo being calculated. Mates receipts were signed for the incorrect cargo quantity, and the agents were authorized to sign the bills of lading on behalf of the master on the basis of the mates receipts.

The chief officer discovered his serious error at the next terminal and informed the master, who *immediately told the managers* of the mistake. The agents were contacted and confirmed that the bills of lading had been signed. P & I clubs were advised and attended the ship to view documentation and take statements. The surveyor also attended, and the calculations were reworked to give the correct cargo.

After discussion between the P & I representative, agents, shipper, and receiver, the original bills of lading were destroyed, and new bills, with the correct figures, issued.

If the situation had not been reported in a prompt manner, the subcharterer would have lost freight on the two thousand tonnes of cargo and in turn would have made a claim against the time charter who would have sued the managers. As it was the chief officer/captain lost no time in informing the managers and the situation was amicably resolved.

Mistakes will occur, but it is important that they are reported immediately so that the situation, where possible, can be quickly settled.

Remember. Read. Ask. Tell.

Technical Aspects

While it is possible to study in isolation the various functions involved in shipping operations, e.g., insurance, personnel, safety, maintenance and repairs, voyage planning, etc., practice brings them together in complex and interactive ways.

For example, the legal requirements of surveys are closely related with the commercial surveys required by the ship's classification society and legal manning requirements very much determine the ship owner's calculations on the economic numbers of crew needed to run it efficiently.

Similarly, it is impossible to examine the commercial aspects of ship operations without making some note on the technical aspects that will influence the ship.

Thus, the ship is expected to have a certain crew because of the technical appliances provided on board, or lack of them; while the size of the ship is usually a direct indicator of the number of crew that are to be carried, as is the cargo a direct indication of the training and certification that will be required to man the ship satisfactorily.

Again, modern ship design can improve a ship's capability and money earning capacity. For example, modern efficient engines do not burn so much fuel for the same speed, and this is a prime instance of technology leading commercialism; lower fuel cost mean lower chartering rates and probably employment in a marginal situation.

Carefully planned maintenance and ship repairs will provide a ship that is capable of carrying out its task, downtime free, and this in turn will mean less penalties for the shipowner, which, in time, will gain him a name for reliability and efficiency.

The shipowner must, therefore, build into a ship's schedule a predetermined planned maintenance program. This may include a certain number of days where the ship will be immobile and not able to work, but given notice, a charterer can plan his schedule, and with a little give-and-take on both sides, the ship can complete a regular maintenance program at a time of less disruption to the charterer.

Obviously any safety repairs should not be held up for commercial or any other reason.

Thus, technical factors will have a direct and significant impact on the commercial viability of ship operations.

Reports and Records

As important as the actual technical aspects of ship management are, the checks that are associated with them are equally vital.

Strict, detailed accounts of all events that affect the ship and its operation should be kept by the ship and shore staff allocated to the ship.

There can be nothing more infuriating for a ship owner to have his ship dry-dock for planned repairs and maintenance and to find that the ship has sustained some major indentation or other damage for which there is no report or record.

Insurance will often refuse to pay for such unreported damage, and it is left to the shipowner to bear the cost of repair or replacement.

Ship's crew should be encouraged to report all instances of accidents and events affecting ship operations, no matter how trivial, using a clearly established company reporting procedure.

This information should then be collated and disseminated by a member of the shore staff to all interested personnel.

This, of course, must not be restricted to ship accidents, but it should be extended to accidents to all persons, both crew and ship visitors, e.g., dockers.

Expenditure Control

These technical reports and records have themselves obvious financial implications in the form of expenditure control.

Ships use a vast array and amount of spare parts, consumables, and equipment, and keeping track of the oil consumption or how many pencils a ship uses is a daunting task unless a complete system of accounting is provided. Many modern companies now use computer technology to control spare parts, maintenance, and purchasing, for example AMOS-D.

In this age of fluctuating demand for ships and shipping, the ship manager should be cost conscious, because a dollar saved on the cost of running the ship could provide the difference between a contract being viable or not.

Many computer systems exist to assist with good bookkeeping and accounting, and an efficient shipping company will provide the minimum amount of paperwork for its ship staff to produce a complete record of all goods and stores received and how they were used.

This information should provide the basis of a budget for the next period of operation and ship master, ship manager, and shipowner should watch the buildup of variances and differences between the actual and budgeted amounts to see if there is any way of reducing expenditures and providing a more economical ship operation that still lies well within the limits of safety.

Reporting Incidents

In the event of any incident that could result in a claim against the company or vessel, a full report must be completed in a recognized P & I or company format.

The details of log entries, shoreside reports, and personal statements must be supported by as much physical evidence as possible.

These evidence will be photographs and drawings of the location (try to introduce some indication of scale in the photograph—a ruler or hand/man), videos (if possible, of surroundings and relevant details), samples (e.g., rope that parted, damaged material/components, etc.).

All this information and support material must be forwarded immediately to the company.

Cooperation with the local authorities is desirable, but ensure that all crew are given access to local legal advice through the P & I correspondent where necessary.

Failure to provide detailed information could affect the company's ability to refute a claim at a later date.

It is, therefore, vital to relate the technical and commercial aspects of a ship's program to come up with the total picture of ship operations that will enable the manager to control an efficient and profitable organization.

Maritime insurance

It is a common tenet that a loss will lie, at the first instance, with the owner. Thus, if a ship sinks and is lost or if cargo is damaged, the owner of the ship and the cargo will bear the costs of the loss.

It may be that the loss or damage was caused by the negligence of another party to the contract or venture; in that case, the person suffering the loss may be able to obtain recompense or damages through the courts or arbitration. A shipowner whose ship was sunk by a collision may try to gain compensation because the navigation of the other ship was at fault. The cargo owner may attempt to gain restitution from the shipowner for the cargo damaged or lost by the actions of the crew of the ship. Unfortunately, for the person suffering the loss or damage in both these cases, the offending shipowner can claim either no liability for damage or limited liability under a convention or national law (e.g., collision—1976 maritime liability convention and cargo damage—Hague-Visby Rules).

Therefore, both the shipowner and the cargo owner would be imprudent to embark on a voyage without providing some form of cover to offset financial losses that could be encountered during the trip.

There are four broad areas of indemnifying the person who has suffered a loss:

- Marine insurance
- General average
- P & I clubs
- Shipowner's liability

Marine insurance in the United Kingdom is covered by the Marine Insurance Act 1906 and by the use of insurance policies, usually contracted with underwriters, that incorporate the institute clauses.

General average is covered by the York-Antwerp Rules (1974) and concerns contributions by all participants of a venture for a loss suffered by an individual for the common good of the voyage.

P & I clubs are organizations where shipowners join together to spread the cost of an individual company's loss or expense.

Shipowner's liability can be categorized into two distinct areas:

- Full liability
- Limited liability

Full liability is where the shipowner will have to pay full compensation for the loss or damage that has occurred.

Limited liability allows the shipowner to pay a percentage of the compensation claimed; this is provided for by statute, convention, or contractual clause.

Average

Frequently, in insurance, the word *average* is encountered; in this context, the term has the meaning of a "loss."
Average can be divided into two areas:

- Particular average
- General average

Particular Average

"Particular average is the incidence of a partial loss or damage of ship, cargo or freight, through unavoidable accident, upon the individual owners (or insurers) of the interest affected" (*Oxford Concise Dictionary*).

It is further defined as "a particular average loss is a partial loss of the subject matter insured, caused by a peril insured against, and which is not a general average loss" (s. 64, Marine Insurance Act 1906).

Common examples of particular average on a ship are heavy weather damage, damage caused by stranding, collision, and fire.

Particular average is normally covered by a marine insurance policy, held with a marine underwriter, which extends to total as well as partial loss.

General Average

General average is the apportionment of loss caused by intentional damage to the ship, sacrifice of cargo, etc. And the expenses incurred to secure the general safety of the ship and cargo.

There is a General Average Act where any extraordinary sacrifice or expenditure is voluntarily and reasonably made or incurred in time of peril for the purpose of preserving the property imperiled in the common adventure (s. 66, MIA 1906).

In the event of an incident of general average, contributions are made to those suffering the loss by all those involved in the voyage.

The principle of general average contributions is peculiar to the law of the sea and extends only to sea risk (*Morrison SS Co. v. Greystoke Castle* (1947)).

The extent of the contribution is based on the value of the participants' interest in the voyage.

Marine Insurance

Although there is no legal compulsion to insure ships or cargoes, the amount of capital involved and the enormous financial losses that may follow a marine casualty make it imprudent to leave risks uninsured.

In the United Kingdom, all present-day marine insurance contracts are governed by the 1906 Marine Insurance Act, where a contract of marine insurance is one that the insurer undertakes to indemnify the assured, in manner and to the extent that has been agreed, against marine losses that are the outcome of a marine adventure (s. 1).

No person is allowed to enter into a contract of marine insurance unless they have an "insurable interest"; this is to reduce the incidents of gaming and wagering on a voyage's outcome, a practice that renders all marine insurance contracts void (s. 4 MIA) and illegal (s. 1 (gambling policies) Marine Insurance Act 1909).

This act provides that any person who effects a contract of marine insurance without having any bona fide interest, direct or indirect, either in the safe arrival of the ship or in the preservation of the subject matter insured, or any person in the employment of the owner of the ship who effects a contract "without further proof of interest than the policy itself" (i.e., PPI) shall be deemed to be gambling on the ship or cargo's loss and shall be liable, on summary conviction, to imprisonment with or without hard labor (s. 1); unfortunately, the United Kingdom authorities abolished hard labor in 1948!

Insurance is effected through a "market," for example, the London Market, which is part of the much larger British insurance industry or markets in the USA, Japan, France, etc.

The London Market specializes in covering major or complex risks, that is, risks incurred by businesses rather than by individuals and private consumers.

The market is characterized by the use of "brokers," who are the commercial marketing arm of the industry and whose function is to seek out the best cover for their customer's needs.

Insurance Procedure

When a shipowner buys a ship or needs to renew his annual insurance premium or a cargo owner requires to have his goods insured for the forthcoming voyage, he usually asks his broker to find insurance cover.

The broker prepares a "slip," which is a document giving a description of the item to be covered, with attendant details of time, location, value, and any other relevant information regarding the risk.

The broker then approaches an acknowledged underwriter (leader) of this category of risk, be it ship, cargo, or whatever, and asks for

- A quote of price of premium
- The percentage of the risk that he is prepared to cover

If, as normally happens, the leader only covers a percentage of the risk, the broker must complete the coverage by showing the insurance to other underwriters (units), who will assess the risk in terms of the premium and percentage quoted by the leader before making their own proposal.

By offering the slip around in this manner allows the risk to be spread and the affects of a loss will be shared among a larger number of underwriters, thus a claim can be met quickly without jeopardizing the security of one insurer. Some risks, such as hull and marine oil platforms, can be "coinsured" between more than fifty separate underwriting units and in addition may even be shared internationally between any number of markets.

When the broker has succeeded in placing the total amount of the risk, he sends a cover note to his client, either shipowner or cargo owner, as confirmation and prepares the final documentation of the transaction, showing the exact share of the risk undertaken by each unit and giving a clear indication of the cover finally agreed.

The contract of insurance is placed between the two principals, the assured (shipowner) and the insurer (underwriter). The marine insurance broker is the professional intermediary and is the agent for the assured.

The presentation of the slip by the broker constitutes the offer, and the writing of each line constitutes an acceptance of this offer (*General Reinsurance Corp. v. Ffp* (1983)).

An underwriting unit can be from two different areas:

- Insurance company
- Lloyd's syndicate

Insurance Company

An insurance company underwrites on the strength of reserves put up by the company. It operates through a department of the company called an underwriting room and services its finances and achieves stability by spreading its total reserves over many classes of business, e.g., motor, housing, property, as well as the marine fields of ships and cargo.

In the United Kingdom, statutory protection for the public supervision of insurance companies is provided for under the Insurance Companies Act (1982).

The act provides a comprehensive scheme to ensure that no one launches or conducts affairs in insurance without sufficient funds to meet claims, expected or unexpected.

Probably one of the best known marine organizations, Lloyd's is a society incorporated by act of Parliament in 1871, which has approximately 33,500 members formed into over 376 syndicates.

Lloyd's Syndicate

A Lloyd's syndicate is an agency whose resources are provided for by the individuals (names of members) that make up the syndicate.

Syndicates transact insurance for their own account and at their own risk. The members of a syndicate have an unlimited liability for paying out claims.

Each syndicate operates under the professional control and authorization of Lloyd's. Though Lloyd's itself does not engage in underwriting, it provides logistical backup, premises, and a reserve fund for its syndicates.

Because of the high esteem to which Lloyd's is held, their members are exempt from the provisions of the Insurance Companies Act.

Some of the larger ship- and cargo-owning companies use a system of insurance that retains most of the financing of loss within the company.

Captive Insurance

Captive insurance operates through an insurance company that is a subsidiary of the parent ship or cargo owning concern; the risk is then written through the subsidiary as if it were an independent organization. Thus the premiums are paid to the subsidiary and do not leave the overall finances of the company.

Though the parent company will have to bear the losses of any claims received, either by its own ships and, of course, from third parties, e.g., after a collision.

Some captive insurance is processed through established insurance companies, but most of the underwriting is then placed with the captive subsidiary company.

The benefits of a company using an insurance company in this way are that

- the captive insurance company has an established worldwide network of agents to oversee claims
- the documents issued are those of a recognized insurance company
- initial general average agreements can be made by a GA guarantee

No Insurance

As already stated, it is not a legal requirement to have hull or cargo insurance; indeed the only statutory insurance required is for tankers that carry over 2,000 DWT of cargo for oil pollution compensation.

Some ship/cargo organizations operate totally without underwriting risks. This could be because of the cost of the premium of the risk, e.g., due to age or condition of the ship or because the company feels that insurance is uneconomic.

Cargo owners may feel that the protection afforded by the Hague/Hague-Visby/Hamburg Rules is sufficient.

Insurance Policy

The final documentation that is produced for the insured risks is called a policy.

The policy consists of the following:

- An outer cover
- A clause inserts depending on the risk

The out cover contains the name of the insuring organization, company, broker, or syndicate.

It further contains the name of the insured, the ship's name and the time period or voyage covered.

Information is also entered on the subject matter insured, e.g., cargo, and its agreed value.

The premium paid is included, as is the name of the company to notify in the event of a loss and where the agreed claims are to be paid.

Finally, any additional clauses, endorsements, special conditions, or warranties are to be entered.

Institute Clauses

Fixed to the outer cover is an insert with the contractual obligations that apply to this policy.

To harmonize the insurance industry, every insurance company and every ship/cargo concern is operating equally, central trade associations, e.g. the Institute of London Underwriters, developed standard clauses for insertion in the policy.

These would provide clauses that were known and understood throughout the market as a suitable general level of cover to be provided to any assured.

Such standard clauses could, of course, be tailored to particular requirements, with cover added or taken away depending on the price and the nature of the risk, but they would act as a common starting point and give a degree of certainty to both the insurer and the insured that might otherwise be lacking.

The major division of institute clauses is between the hull (for ships) and cargo.

The range of subjects that are covered by the institute cargo clauses are as varied as the cargoes that a ship can carry:

- Institute cargo clauses
- Institute timber trade federation clauses
- Institute strike clauses
- Institute jute clauses
- Etc.

Basically they are all very much the same and include clauses on:

- *Navigation.* It provides that the ship is covered at all times, may sail with or without pilots, and can assist and tow ships in distress.
- *Breach of warranty.* Used to be called held covered, it covers the ship for a breach of the fundamental conditions of the contract as long as the underwriters were given immediate notice of the breach and the policy was amended and any additional premiums required were paid.
- *Termination.* The insurance will automatically end at the time of change of classification society, expiration of class, change of flag, or transfer to new management.
- *Perils.* These are the accepted areas where the shipowner will be covered for loss, and it includes maritime perils, fire, explosion, piracy, contact with aircraft, earthquake, negligence of master, officers, crew, or pilot.
- *Pollution hazard.* The insurance covers loss of or damage to the ship caused by any government authority acting to prevent or mitigate a pollution hazard; this covers the shipowner for incidents where the ship is destroyed under the intervention convention regulations, such as the *Torrey Canyon* incident where the UK government bombed a tanker that was leaking oil (1966).

- *Three-fourths collision liability.* It is also known as the *running down clause*, where the underwriters agree to indemnify the insured for three-quarters of any sum paid out for damage caused by loss or damage to another ship, etc.
- *Sistership.* This clause allows ships of the same company to be treated as if they were of different companies with regard to collision and salvage.
- *Notice of claims and tenders.* In the event of an incident where loss or damage has been sustained and a claim may result, notice must be given to the underwriters prior to survey so that they may appoint their own surveyor and repair yard.

Failure to observe this clause could result in a deduction of 15 percent of the ascertained claim.

- *General average and salvage.* The insurance covers the ship's proportion of salvage, salvage charges, and/or general average.
- *Deductible.* No claims arising from a peril insured against shall be payable unless the aggregate of all such claims exceeds an agreed sum.
- *Duty of assured.* Originally known as *sue and labor*, and it is included to emphasize that the shipowner, master, etc., take such measures as may be reasonable for the purpose of averting or minimizing a loss that could be recoverable under the policy.
- *New for old.* Claims are payable without a deduction for new for old.
- *Constructive total loss.* There is a constructive total loss when the cost of salvaging, repairing, or recovering the insured risk is greater than the value of the risk.
- *War exclusion.* Generally policies do not cover ships for damage caused by war, civil war, revolution, etc., nor damage caused by derelict mines, torpedoes, or bombs; thus a ship entering a known warzone will require a new policy at a higher premium.
- Finally, insurance cover does not normally extend to damage caused by strikers, lockout, terrorists, or any weapon of war or nuclear fission/fusion.

General Average

General average is an ancient concept and dates back to the Rhodian Law of two thousand years ago (*Digest of Justinian*).

It involves a system where all those persons having a financial interest in a venture (voyage) pay a contribution to someone who has suffered an intentional loss or expense to save the outcome of the voyage.

It was stated in one of the earliest English cases in which the principal of general average was recognized that "all loss which arises in consequence of extraordinary sacrifices made or expenses incurred for the preservation of the ship and cargo comes within general average, and must be borne proportionally by all who are interested" (*Birkley v. Presgrave* (1801))

General average on board a ship is applied and administered under the internationally recognized York-Antwerp Rules (1974).

Though general average is a custom that has been accepted for countless years, it is still necessary to include a clause in a contract to implement the York-Antwerp Rules into a specific agreement:

> General average to be settled according to York-Antwerp Rules (1974). Proprietors of cargo to pay the cargo's share in general average even if same has been necessitated through neglect or default of the owner's servants (Clause 11, Gen Con).

The York-Antwerp rules lay down the conditions that must apply before losses and expenditures come under general average and how contributions are to be calculated and paid.

York-Antwerp Rules (1994)

The rules consist of two sections:

- Lettered rules (a–g)
- Numbered rules (i–xxii)

In the Makis case, it was ruled that the Y-A Rules were intended to be a complete code, the lettered section having precedence and setting out the general principles and the numbered section being referred to in particular instances. This concept was included in the 1974 rules as the rule of interpretation (neither letter nor number): "In the adjustment of general average the following lettered and numbered rules shall apply . . . Except as provided by the numbered rules, general average shall be adjusted according to the lettered rules."

General average is to be adjusted according to the lettered rules, and the basic principles of adjustment is defined as "there is a general average act when, and only when, any extraordinary sacrifice or expenditure is intentionally and reasonably made or incurred for the common safety for the purpose of preserving from peril the property involved in a common maritime adventure" (rule a).

This principle has been accepted throughout the ages that general average losses must arise from a deliberate sacrifice, with the reasonable intention of preserving the ship and its cargo (*The Bona* (1895)).

The main conditions for an act, sacrifice, or expenditure to qualify for general average are as follows:

- The venture must be maritime (*Morrison SS Co v. Greystoke Castle* (1947)).
- The act must be voluntarily made, i.e., is intentional (*McCall v. Houlder Bros.* (1897); s. 66, MIA (1906)).
- The act must result from the action of man, not the fortuitous result of ordinary and normal perils of the sea (*Birkley v. Presgrave* (1801)).
- The act must be reasonable (*The Seapool* (1934)) and necessary (s. 66, MIA (1906)).
- Sacrifice and expense must be of an extraordinary nature (*Société Nouvelle d'Armement v. Spillers & Bakers Ltd.* (1917); 66 MIA (1906)).

- Sacrifice and expenditure must be made or incurred in the time of peril (*Joseph Watson & Son Ltd. v. Fireman's Fund Insurance Co.* (1922); s. 66, MIA (1906)), though the peril need not be immediate (*McCall v. Houlder Bros.* (1897)), it must be real (*The West Imboden* (1936)).

It must be for the purpose of preserving the property imperiled in the common adventure (*Kemp v. Halliday* (1866)).

- The interests concerned must be involved in a common adventure (the J. P. Donaldson (1897); *Dabney v. New England Co.* (1867)).
- The sacrifice or expenditure must achieve success (*Chellew v. Royal Commission on the Sugar Supply* (1921)).

The acts that incur general average costs can be divided into two categories:

- Acts of sacrifice
- Acts of expenditure

Sacrifice

Sacrifice is incurred when the subject matter is intentionally destroyed or lost; this can include the following:

- Jettison of cargo, when it is carried in accordance with a recognized custom of the trade (rule i).

The master has a right to exercise this power in case of imminent dangers (*The Gratitudine* (1801)) and against Deck Cargo (*Gould v. Oliver* (1837)).

- Damage to machinery and boilers of a ship, which is ashore and in a position of peril, in endeavoring the refloat (rule vii)
- Voluntary stranding when a ship is intentionally run ashore for the common safety of the venture (rule v)

- Damage to the ship or cargo due to efforts to extinguish a fire (rule iii)
- Cutting away wreck (rule iv) and ship's cargo, material and stores used as fuel (rule ix).

Expenditure

Expenditure is the extraordinary costs sustained in preserving the property of all concerned in the adventure.

- Salvage remuneration, under contract or otherwise, incurred saving all the interests in the adventure to the extent that the salvage operations were undertaken for the purpose of preserving from peril the property involved in the common maritime venture (rule vi).
- Expenses lightening the ship when ashore, with regard to cargo, ship's stores and fuel (rule viii).
- Expenses at a port of refuge necessary for the common safety; this can include the expenses of entering and leaving, the cost of handling cargo on board, the costs of discharging, storing and reloading cargo, stores and fuel, the additional insurance while the cargo is ashore. *All this being necessary for the damage to the ship, caused by the sacrifice or accident, to be repaired* (rule x).
- Loss of freight arising from the damage to, or loss of, cargo (rule xv).

General Average Adjustments

When a general average act has incurred a sacrifice or expenditure, the cost of this must be borne by all those who had an interest in the voyage.

The parties that have an interest can include the shipowner, charterer, cargo owner, and on some occasions, the freight holder.

The calculation of each individual's general average contribution is made by the average adjuster, an independent arbitrator selected by the various interests.

The contribution is based on the actual net value of the property at the termination of the adventure (rule xvii).

It is the duty of the master to collect the general average contributions from the respective parties to the adventure, even where the sacrifice was cargo (*Strang v. Scott* (1889)).

The shipowner is liable in damages to the owner of goods jettisoned if he delivers the rest of the cargo without obtaining general average security.

It cannot be too strongly emphasized that an appropriate security must always be obtained by a master before the delivery of any cargo.

Security

The shipowner has a common law lien on cargo for general average (*Hingston v. Wendt* (1876)).

It is not normal for the shipowner to exercise this lien, but before letting the cargo out of his possession, the master should obtain some form of agreement or security for the general average contribution, this can be as follows:

- Cash payment for the expected amount, when the general average contribution is not too great
- General average bond, which is a contract between the shipowner and the contributor that the full proportion of general average contribution will be paid on demand
- General average deposit, which will be made in conjunction with the GA bond; it represents a percentage of the provisional amount of general average.
- Average guarantee is made by underwriters of cargo insurance and is an agreement to pay the full proportion of general average on demand when it has been calculated.

When one of the securities has been obtained, the ship will release the cargo to the consignee, and at a later date, when the final adjustments have been made, the shipowner will receive the full amounts on surrender of the security.

Protection and Indemnity (P & I)

Protection and indemnity associations, commonly referred to as P & I clubs, were formed in the United Kingdom from 1855 onward by shipowners for their mutual protection against those risks which were not covered under ordinary marine insurance, either hull or cargo, e.g.,

- The last quarter damage sustained in collision
- Loss from nondelivery of cargo
- Crew repatriation costs
- Third-party liability for personal injury to passengers and crew

There are over a dozen P & I clubs in the United Kingdom, and there many others to be found in Scandinavia, the United States, and Japan.

In the United Kingdom, the clubs are as follows:

- Run on a nonprofit-making mutual entry fee basis
- Controlled by committees of representatives of the shipowner members
- Managed by experts who calculate the fees due, collect the premiums from the members and deal with claims as they arise

The claims on the association, of which the majority are in connection with passenger, crew, and cargo, are met by financial "calls" on the members at annual intervals, though further calls can be made at intermediate dates as the occasion demands, and, in rare instances, refunds are made.

Thus, in one year, the liabilities and claims of a member may be heavy, and in consequence, the call on all members might be higher than normally experienced.

The amount of the individual call is traditionally based on the gross tonnage of each ship the member has in the club.

P & I clubs in the United Kingdom include shipowners from all parts of the world and foreign flag ships are represented on the committees.

In recent years, many clubs have been formed for diversified sectors of the marine industry:

- Protection against bad debts (ITIC)
- Small ships (the shipowners)
- Strike cover (Transmarine Mutual Strike Assurance Association)
- Etc.

Generally, the P & I clubs are either arranged geographically or by trade, providing protection.

Protection

This covers subjects including the following:

- Loss of life
- Collision or damage to another ship or fixed object crew expenses, including repatriation, sickness, and funerals abroad
- Government inquiries
- Raising and removing wrecks (probably the most expensive item that P & I will attempt)

Indemnity

This covers shipowner's

- Liability through contracts
- Liabilities to cargo interests
- Custom fines for innocent breaches of regulations
- Cost of fighting cases
- Proportion of general average when in excess of the insured value

Freight covers the legal cost of recovering freight and other cargo related dues such as demurrage.

War risks covers mine damage risks, and in the event of hostilities, it would cover the shipowner until the ship reached a port of refuge and/or a government war-risk scheme could be introduced.

Other—The P & I club provide a final indispensable service of administration:

- Posting bond for arrested ships
- Disseminating information, e.g., new legislation regarding pollution
- Advising their members on suspect commercial practices and how to avoid their dire consequences
- Producing lists of acceptable lawyers, surveyors, and advisors
- Producing standard forms of letters, e.g., of indemnity, protest, etc.

P & I provides the benefit of the economies of scale; larger shipping companies can absorb the expenses of noninsured items by spreading the cost around its fleet.

However, the smaller ship-owning company needs the protection afforded by the club as it spreads these noninsured costs that have been incurred around all its members.

Liability

Shipowner's Liability

Wherever a ship carries cargo that is lost or damaged or discharges oil that pollutes a coastline or strikes another ship or structure, there may be a degree of responsibility for making good the loss, repairing the damage, or restoring the environment.

Whether this is a full replacement cost or a reduced payment will depend on the circumstances of the case as will the fact that the shipowner may have no liability whatsoever for the damage or loss.

Under various international conventions and national laws, this liability is defined as follows:

- Excluded
- Limited
- Full

Excluded liability is when the incident that caused the loss falls under a section of the law that allows the shipowner to escape any responsibility for payment or reimbursement, e.g.,

- Cargo (Hague-Visby), act of god, Queen's enemies, etc.
- Pollution (International Convention on Civil Liability for Oil Pollution (1969) (CLC), act or omission done with intent to cause damage by a third party
- Passenger's luggage (Athens Convention), carrier shall not be liable for the loss or damage to monies, negotiable securities, gold, silver, etc., except where such valuables have been deposited with the carrier for safekeeping.

Limited liability is where an incident causes loss or damage, and it falls within the shipowner's normal operation; thus, he is able to invoke the regulations contained in the convention/law to protect himself against full reimbursement of the loss.

Under the regulations, the shipowner can reduce the amount payable to the person suffering the loss to an agreed amount based on the weight of the cargo or the gross tonnage of the ship.

Examples of possible limitations of liability are as follows:

- *Cargo.* With all the exceptions from liability that are available, the shipowner is only liable to pay a limited amount where the management of cargo has caused loss or damage (Hague-Visby).
- *Pollution.* Oil tanker owner can limit his liability where the damage was caused by an accidental spill of oil from a collision or grounding (CLC (1969)).

- *General.* Claims with respect to loss of life or loss of or damage to property occurring on board or in direct connection with the operation of the ship (Maritime Claims Convention (1976)).
- *Passengers.* The carrier shall be liable for the damage suffered as a result of the death of or personal injury to passengers (Athens Convention).

Limitation is allowed up to the specified amounts.

- Hague-Visby   666.67 SDR per package or 2 SDR per kilo
- CLC   133 SDR per GT up to 14 million SDR
- Maritime Claims   167,000 SDR for a ship with tonnage not exceeding 500 GT
- Athens   46,666 SDR per passenger

Full liability occurs when there is some factor that negates the protection afforded by the convention or law, and the shipowner then experiences the full force of compensation and reimbursement.

Frequently full liability is activated by the shipowner's lack of due diligence in carrying out his ship operations.

- *Cargo.* The carrier shall be bound before and at the beginning of the voyage to exercise due diligence to make the ship seaworthy, properly manned, equipped and supplied, and make all parts in which cargo is to be carried fit and safe for their reception (HV art. 3 (1)); failure to comply with this article will remove the limitation of liability cover from the shipowner.
- *Pollution.* The tanker owner may not avail himself of the limitation of liability for oil pollution damage if the incident occurred as a consequence of the actual fault of, or of someone in privity with, the owner (CLC).
- *General.* A person liable shall not be entitled to limit his liability if it is proved that the loss resulted from his personal act or omission, committed with intent to cause such loss or recklessly and with knowledge that such loss would probably result (Maritime Claims, art. 4).

- *Passenger.* The carrier shall not be entitled to benefit from the limitation of liability if it is proved that the damage resulted from an act or omission of the carrier done with intent to cause damage or recklessly and with knowledge that such damage would probably result (Athens, art. 13).

Adjustments for General Average

When a general average act has incurred a sacrifice or expenditure, the cost of this must be borne by all those who had an interest in the voyage.

The parties that have an interest and thus can be expected to contribute to general average include the following:

- The shipowner
- Charterer
- Cargo owner
- Freight holder
- Contractors that have hired navigational or radio equipment to the shipowner

The contribution is based on the actual net value of the property at the termination of the adventure (rule xvii).

In the case of cargo, the starting point would be the invoice value of the goods, but there may have been a sudden market fluctuation, which would increase or decrease their saleable value. In this case, it would be this value less damage or loss that would be taken into account.

Collection of GA Contributions

It is the duty of a specialist on behalf of the ship to collect the general average contributions from the respective parties to the adventure.

The shipowner is liable in damages to the owner of goods jettisoned if he delivers the rest of the cargo without obtaining general average security.

It cannot be too strongly emphasized that an appropriate security must always be obtained by a master before the delivery of any cargo.

The shipowner has a common law lien on cargo for general average (*Hingston v. Wendt* (1876)).

It is not normal for the shipowner to exercise this lien, but before letting the cargo out of his possession, the master should obtain some form of agreement or security for the general average contribution; this can be as follows:

- Cash payment
- General average bond
- General average deposit
- Average guarantee
- Or any combination of these

When one of the securities has been obtained, the ship will release the cargo to the consignee, and at a later date, when the final adjustments have been made, the shipowner will receive the full amounts on surrender of the security.

Nonseparation Agreement

A problem can arise with regard to cargo that is either off loaded at the time of the incident or discharged at a port of refuge and not reloaded, either because the port is the cargoes' destination or it is forwarded by some other means.

This is covered by a nonseparation agreement, such that in the event of cargo not being returned to the ship, the rights and liabilities under general average are not affected.

When a shipper's cargo is loaded into lighters from a stranded ship and is taken straight to its destination, the rights and liabilities involved in this are not affected as a nonseparation agreement is in force.

Similarly, any discharged cargo at the port of refuge that is transferred by road to its destination would still be liable for GA contributions and should not be released until some form of security is arranged.

Where the contribution is large, the shipowner would be advised to secure either

- GA bond and GA deposit or
- GA bond and GA guarantee

In the case of most smaller cargoes, they are shipped with insurance, CIF, and the GA guarantee would probably be sufficient.

However, where there is no insurance, the shipowner is advised to hold the cargo until some payment is made.

Claims for Liability

Claims against a ship can be classed as follows:

- Collision/loss of ship
- Personal injury
- Cargo loss and delay
- Pollution

Collision/Loss of Ship

A shipowner will argue that the collision occurred as part of both ships' fault or even that it was entirely the other vessel's fault and try to get some kind of redress.

If they cannot apportion blame to the other vessel, they will then attempt to limit their liability under the flag states version of the Maritime Claims Convention (1976) as a loss or damage to property in direct connection with the operation of the ship (article 2).

If the vessel was obviously to blame, the other vessel's owners will attempt to place full liability on the vessel by suggesting that it is barred by its conduct from limiting liability due to personal act or omission committed with intent to cause loss or recklessly and with knowledge that such loss would result (article 4).

They could do this by showing that the unsafe operation of the ship was known to the company; that they were to be judged by the standard of conduct of the ordinary, reasonable, shipowner in the management and control of ships; that the primary concern of a shipowner was safety of life at sea; and that involved a seaworthy ship, properly manned and safely navigated (Lady Gwendolen 1966).

Similarly it could be argued that the company failed to ensure the ship was manned with competent officers, and they further failed to supervise and check on how their ship was navigated, especially in fog (The Garden City 1982).

Thus when it can be shown that the watch officer was known to have a drinking problem and no action had been taken, or it can be shown that the master had no operational guidelines regarding incapable or incompetent officers, traffic separation, fog, etc., or that his actions had never been monitored or supervised in a clear, precise, and comprehensive manner (*The Marion* (1983)).

It will be extremely difficult for the shipowner or ship manager to claim that the events leading up to a collision occurred without his fault and privity, and therefore no limitation of liability would probably be allowed.

Injury to Crew

Injury to a seaman will be approached along similar lines and under the same national legislation prepared from the Maritime Claims Convention (1976) (article 2).

Cargo Loss or Damage

Cargo claims can be divided into two categories:

- Claims for loss and damage
- Claims for delay

The main provisions for cargo loss and damage are to be found in the Hague or Hague-Visby Rules. These provide that when the carrier, who could be the shipowner or a charterer, exercises due diligence before and at the beginning of the voyage to

- Make the ship seaworthy
- Properly man, equip, and supply the ship
- Make the holds, etc., fit and safe for the reception, carriage, and preservation of cargo (HV, article iii)

Then neither he nor the ship shall be liable for loss or damage (article iv (1)).

This makes it very difficult for the cargo-owning claimant or his insurer to gain any recompense for cargo loss or damage.

The rules provide that it is for the claimant to show that a loss was caused by one of the above, and only then, with regard to unseaworthiness, does the carrier have the burden of proving the exercise of due diligence (HV, article iv).

For example

- If the steering gear broke down, but the shipowner had shown due diligence by including a spare, which had, unfortunately, proved ineffective. Were the shipowners to know that it would work? Of course not; therefore, how can they be penalized. If they had a habit of selecting shoddy spares, it may be a different story.
- If a collision occurred as a peril, danger, or accident of the sea, albeit the ship was obviously in the wrong separation lane, and again, what could the carrier have done at that time, assuming

that he had issued operational orders about safe navigation and previously checked that they had be carried out?
- ♦ If the watch officers had a lack of competence, this would be covered by the section that refers to the carrier not being responsible for loss or damage arising from any act, neglect, or default of the master or servants of the carrier in the navigation or in the management of the ship (Hague-Visby, article iv (2)).
- ♦ Possibly the use of an out-of-date chart, which should have been disposed of, could be termed lack of due diligence on part of the carrier (*The Marion* (1983)).

If the cargo is being carried under the Hamburg Rules, it is harder for the carrier to evade liability because the carrier is liable for loss resulting from loss of or damage to the goods, as well as from delay in delivery, if the occurrence which caused the loss, damage, or delay took place while the goods were in his charge. Unless the carrier proves that he, his servants, or agents took all measures that could reasonably be required to avoid the occurrence and its consequences (article 5).

Is it any wonder why few shipping companies would want to use contracts of carriage that come under the auspices of the Hamburg Rules?

When cargo is not being carried under Hamburg (which is on most occasions), claims for compensation related to the delay of cargo being delivered are dealt with the Maritime Claims Convention (1976) (article 2 (1) (b)), with all the attendant limitations and exclusions discussed above.

Pollution

Oil Tankers

Compensation and cleanup costs for all aspects of pollution play a large part in today's ship management.

For all vessels, the cost of cleanup of an oil spill either from an incident or from daily operation, such as bunkering, can be enormous, and somebody has to pay.

All tank vessels, with over two thousand tonnes of cargo, trading to CLC countries have compulsory insurance. They require a certificate to prove that they have sufficient cover (usually through P & I) for the size of the vessel.

In addition, many countries (and charterers) insist on additional P & I cover of $600 million for incidents.

Non-Tankers

A vessel that is not a tanker has no obligation under the compensation regulations of CLC and the FC.

Obviously, someone needs to clean polluted beaches, and the local population will need compensation for lost livelihoods.

The most likely recourse for claiming against loss is through the Maritime Claims Convention (1976); this, however, allows the shipowner to limit his liability, with the same provisos regarding fault, privity, and due diligence.

Non-Oil Pollution

Regarding pollution, the rules of the Maritime Claims Convention (MCC) only exclude claims for oil pollution damage that come within the meaning of the International Convention on Civil Liability for Oil Pollution (1969) (CLC).

Therefore, all other pollution from hazardous materials, chemicals, etc., must be dealt with through MCC.

US Oil Pollution Act of 1990 (OPA)

One country that has decided to provide its own legislation regarding oil and non-oil pollution compensation and cleanup is the United States of America.

Under OPA *all* vessels have a responsibility to provide cleanup organizations in the event of a pollution incident. Tankers must provide a written plan called a vessel response plan (VRP) that gives details of the proposed contracted organizations.

Also under OPA, *all* vessels must provide certificates of financial responsibility (COFR) covering the limit of their liability. These COFR must be placed with responsible financial organizations that can prove they have necessary backing.

COFR covers the vessel's obligation under OPA and also under CERCLA the US legislation regarding compensation and cleanup of non-oil pollution, e.g., chemical incidents.

Lien

Lien is the right in law of one person to retain in his possession property belonging to another until the claims of the person in possession against the other are satisfied.

It is an efficient method for obtaining payment for outstanding debts or claims that another person wishes to ignore.

The property held by the person enforcing the lien is lost to its owner for the duration of the lien, and if a ship, it is earning no hire or freight; if cargo, it is unsellable and thus a cash flow liability.

The owner of the thing under lien thus has his attention focused on retrieving his property, and the disagreement will come to a speedy conclusion.

Liens can be categorized as follows:

a. possessory
b. non-possessory

A possessory lien exists where the person seeking satisfaction has actual possession, rightfully obtained, of the property.

This type of lien can arise under the following:

- The common law, when it is known as a legal lien
- A contract agreed by the parties involved, when it is known as an equitable lien or a contractual lien

A non-possessory lien occurs when a claim is held over property that the claimant cannot take into his actual possession because of the property's size, location, or nonavailability.

The most common non-possessory lien is a maritime lien though there are occasions where an equitable lien from participation in a contract can be non-possessory.

A further subdivision of maritime and common law liens (legal liens) is as follows:

- ◆ Particular, which entitles the claimant to retain in respect of charges incurred with regard to the thing possessed only.
- ◆ General, which entitle the claimant to retain possession of the property until all claims of the possessor are satisfied, irrespective of the item the claims are against.

Though liens do occur in a general commercial sense, this section will look at the liens found in shipping operations, and examples will be mainly from shipping law.

Categories of Liens

Possessory Liens

This category of lien can arise where the person in possession of the goods has

- Bestowed labor, skill, or expense in altering and improving the goods
- Been obliged to receive the goods or render the service which has given occasion to the lien
- Saved the goods from loss at sea or capture by an enemy.

At common law, the carrier has provided a service in carrying the goods and, thus, has a particular legal lien on the goods carried in respect of all sums due to him for freight (anonymous (1701)), general average contributions (*Crooks v. Allen* (1879); *The Corinthian Glory* (1977)) which includes salvage costs and money spent protecting the cargo (*Hingston v. Wendt* (1876)).

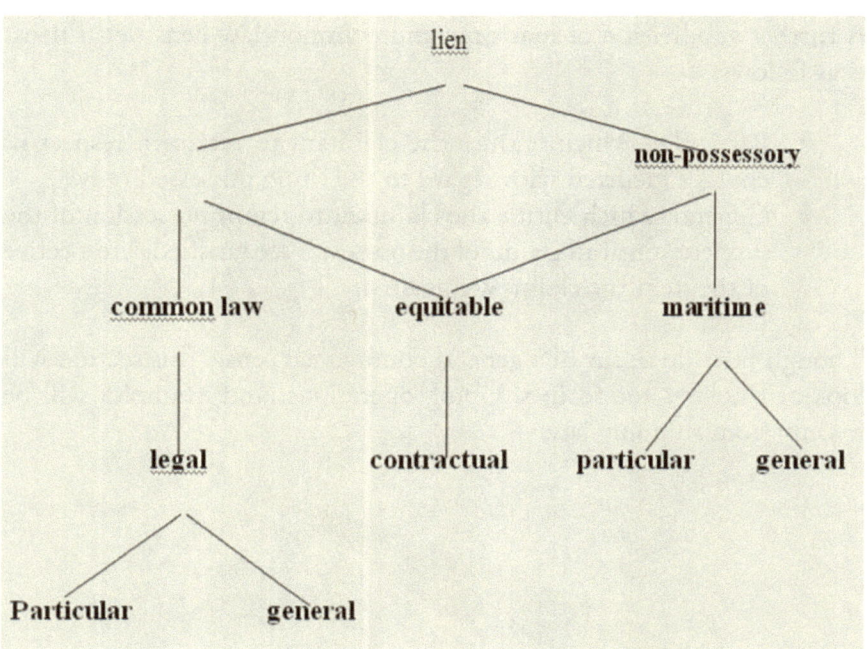

The carrier has no common law lien in respect of any other sums owing to him from the cargo owner in connection with other transactions (*Oppenheim v. Russell* (1802)), for example, dead freight (*Phillips v. Rodie* (1812)), advance freight (*Kirchner v. Venus* (1859)) and demurrage (*Birley v. Gladstone* (1814)).

The carrier may acquire a lien for these and for all other such money due to him by an express term in the contract (*McLean & Hope v. Fleming* (1871)), a particular equitable lien.

The equitable or contractual lien is evidenced by a clause in the charter party: "The owners shall have a lien on the cargo for freight, deadfreight, demurrage, and average contribution due to them under this Charterparty" (NORGRAIN clause 34).

"The carrier shall have a lien over the goods . . . for all freight, primage, charges, demurrage, damages for detention . . . (New Zealand Southbound Trade Bill of Lading (1978), clause 8).

Liens created by contract cover any manner of items the parties to the contract may wish:

- Dead freight
- Demurrage (*Gray v. Carr* (1871); *The Anwar al Sabar* (1980))
- "All sub-freights" (*The Cebu* (1983))
- "Freight, demurrage and all other charges whatsoever," which included warehouse charges (*Harley v. Gardner* (1932))
- Damages for detention.

The carrier has a lien, at common law, not only for freight and general average contributions due for the goods upon which he exercises the lien but for sums due for freight and general average in respect of all goods of the same owner in the same ship on the same voyage, but not against goods on different voyages under different contracts (*Bernal v. Pim* (1835)).

This applies even where the goods are carried under different bills of lading (*Sodergren v. Flight & Jennings* (1796)), a general possessory lien.

If the bill of lading for the goods has been endorsed or delivered to different endorsees, the carrier may not exercise, against one person, a lien in respect of freight and general average contributions due on goods indicated in the bill of lading which has been transferred to another (*Sodergren v. Flight & Jennings* (1796)).

The carrier loses his lien if he delivers the goods to the consignee, unless he was induced to do so by fraud. He may deliver some of the goods on which he has a lien and continue to exercise a lien on other goods which he retains in respect of sums owing (*Bernal v. Pim* (1835)).

If the carrier discharges the goods into a warehouse of a third party, he loses the lien at common law (*Mors-Le Blanch v. Wilson* (1873)) though the lien revives if he obtains possession of the goods once more.

When a carrier discharges the goods into one of his own warehouses, he continues to hold a lien as he is still in possession of the goods (*Mors-Le Blanch v. Wilson* (1873)).

The carrier may also be allowed to sell the goods if a clause to that effect is included into the contract of affreightment: "The carrier shall have a lien over the goods, and the right to sell the same by public auction or otherwise for all freight" (New Zealand Southbound Trade Bill of Lading (1978), clause 8).

Maritime Liens

There are occasions where a ship incurs a debt or a charge is levied against it; in most cases, the shipowner will settle the outstanding amount as there is no dispute as to the charge or the debt.

However, there are times when the shipowner is in dispute with the person bringing the charge and the shipowner will not or cannot settle, or even, the shipowner may not be aware that a charge is due.

In the event of nonpayment or disregard by the shipowner it would be impossible for the creditor or injured party to gain physical possession of the ship.

Thus a system of maritime lien has evolved allowing the claimant the right to have the vessel and cargo seized as security for the outstanding amounts.

A maritime lien travels with the thing to which it attaches, into whosoever hands that thing may pass, it is in no way dependent on possession

A maritime lien is a privileged claim on a ship or on her cargo or on either both these and the freight in respect of service done to or injury caused by them (*The Ripon City* (1897))

A maritime lien cannot generally exist in respect of a foreign-state-owned vessel (*The Parlement Belge* (1880)).

Modern practice is included in the International Convention for the Unification of Certain Rules relating to Maritime Liens and Mortgages (1967); unfortunately insufficient states have ratified this convention to make it operable. Therefore, most legal issues on this subject are settled by national law, one of the most important being the decisions of the Admiralty Court of England.

English law recognizes a limited number of maritime liens:

- Damage done by the ship
- Salvage done to the ship
- Seamen's and master's wages
- Master's disbursements
- Bottomry and respondentia

Maritime liens can be divided into two main categories:

- For damage suffered
- For money due under a contract

Damages suffered include incidents where the vessel has collided with another vessel, a quay, or some other structure; it could also cover damages suffered due to pollution from a non-tanker.

Money due under contract would include situations where the crew are owed wages, a ship's agent has not been paid for services rendered, tug owners wish to hold the vessel until some agreement is found with regard to salvage payment.

Master's disbursements are expenses by the master for items that are necessary for the navigation of the ship and the prosecution of the voyage (*The Orienta* (1895)).

Other examples (albeit very dated) of contracts which allow maritime liens to be placed are as follows:

Respondentia, which is in respect of a loan to the master that enables the vessel to continue on voyage; the security for the loan lies in the cargo.

Bottomry, which is money borrowed by the master on the security of the ship and freight for the purpose of completing the voyage.

To exercise a maritime lien, the claimant must proceed through an action in rem in the admiralty court (Supreme Court Act 1981), where he must satisfy the court that there are good grounds for a claim against the ship.

Once the plaintiff has obtained a writ for the action in rem, he can apply for a warrant to arrest the ship, which is done by a court official "nailing a writ to the main mast."

Another form of restraint is by a Mareva injunction; this forbids the movement of a company's assets from the jurisdiction of the court (*Mareva Compania Naviera SA v. International Bulkcarriers SA* (1975)).

In both the above instances, if the defendant in the case sails his ship (*The Jarlinn* (1965)) or disposes of his assets, he will be held in contempt of court and liable to be imprisoned.

Under a maritime lien, it is possible, after a successful court proceedings, to sell the ship and use the proceeds to settle any outstanding amounts.

Priority of Liens

When the money is paid or the vessel is sold to obtain funds to settle the debts, there will possibly be more than one claimant.

To facilitate this, there has evolved a priority of liens; some countries have this priority written into their national law. In the United Kingdom, there are no statutory provisions setting out the order of priority for maritime claims.

Generally, the order appears to be that contractual maritime liens have precedent over common law possessory liens though discretion for approving priority liens rest solely with the courts.

Contractual liens normally have the order:

Salvage, because successful salvage preserves the property out of which the other claimants can be paid (*The Gustaf* (1862); *The Lyrma No. 2* (1978)).

Competing salvage claims rank in that the most recent claim comes first while the earlier claims come last.

1. Wages, master's and seamen's wages rank equal (*The Royal Wells* (1984))
2. Master's disbursements
3. Bottomry (*The Union* (1860)).

Damage liens all rank equal, even though it can be proved that some occurred before others (The Steam Fisher (1927)). Where there are conflicting claims between contractual and damage liens, the matter is dealt with on an equitable basis, guided by the following principles (*The Inna* (1938)).

1. Maritime liens for negligence (tort) rank prior to those arising from contract which accrued before the tort.

2. Salvage lien attaching to a ship after a collision will take precedence over the damage liens resulting from the collision (*The Inna* (1938)).
3. Wages lien are put after subsequent damage liens and probably after earlier damage liens as well (*The Elin* (1882)).

Discharge of Liens

When a cargo owner wishes to regain his goods or a shipowner decides that he wants the use of his vessel, they both must take steps to satisfy either the possessory lien holder or the court that imposed the maritime lien that they are willing to

1. Pay what is due
2. Come to some mutual agreement
3. Put up a bond for the disputed amount with a court as good faith.

The latter option is possibly the most common, as payment could have been made if there had been prior agreement.

The bond posted can be as follows:

1. A cash payment, to be held in suspense until a trial decides on the merits of the case, and either pays the money to the claimant or returns it to the person who posted it.
2. A bank guarantee for the disputed amount
3. A guarantee from the vessel's P & I club that any outstanding amount will be paid after the court has decided.

The lien holder then releases the cargo or gets the writ lifted from the ship.

The protagonists now resort to law or arbitration for settlement of their disagreement, secure in the knowledge that whatever the outcome, the money will be available.

Salvage

Hopefully a ship will never be in a position to request salvage assistance, nor should masters be encouraged to attempt the salvage of other ships, except possibly their own company ships unless they are purposely built tugs.

Unfortunately salvage does occur, and the rules concerning it form an interesting part of the commercial aspects of ship operations.

Under the 1910 Brussel's Convention for the Unification of Certain Rules of Law Respecting Assistance and Salvage at Sea (Safety Convention), a master of a ship shall render assistance to any person who is found at sea and is in danger of being lost.

The master has an obligation to save life; he is under no obligation to save property.

Saving property is called *salvage* (the remuneration for saving property is also called salvage).

The right of salvage only arises in certain circumstances:

- Maritime property was saved; this includes ships, their apparel, cargo, and wreckage.
- The act took place in tidal waters (*The Goring* (1987)).
- The property was in danger, which was a real danger, such that any prudent master would consider it reasonable to accept an offer of assistance.
- The assistance was voluntary.
- The salvage was successful, i.e., no cure, no pay.

The reward for salvage is determined by either courts or arbitration, and the actual amount will depend on the following:

- The degree of danger to the salvage ship
- The risk and danger to the property saved

- The enterprise of the salvors and the extent of risk to which they were exposed
- The amount of labor and skill applied by the salvors
- The value of the property saved
- The loss, if any, incurred by the salvor

There is no need for a written contract between the salvor and the ship requiring assistance though it is common to use one such as the Lloyd's Open Form (LOF).

On no account should salvage be turned down when a ship is in danger because of the salvors' reluctance to sign an open form or because the salvor is asking for an exorbitant fee as the salvage is judged on the criteria listed above and courts will come to an equitable award.

Lloyd's Open Form

At present, the most widely used salvage agreement is Lloyd's Open Form (1995) (LOF '95).

The advantage of any written contract is that both parties can see, at the time of signing and at a later date when a dispute has arisen, the actual agreement, its provisions, its clauses and penalties.

LOF is so widely used that every ship should carry one, and one should be held on file in the company's offices; thus in any salvage situation, the master and the management will be fully aware of the conditions of the contract.

The major conditions of LOF are as follows:

- The salvor shall use his best endeavors to salve the vessel and its cargo, etc.
- The salvor shall use his best endeavors while performing th salvage service to prevent or minimize damage to the environment.

- Subject to the statutory provisions relating to *special compensation*, the services shall be rendered and accepted as salvage service upon the principle of no cure, no pay.
- The salvor agrees to take the ship to a named port or a place of safety.
- The owners and servants of the salved ship shall cooperate fully with the salvors, allowing them to use ship's equipment, machinery, anchors, etc.
- Remuneration will be fixed by arbitration in London.
- The owners of the ship shall promptly accept redelivery of the salved ship.
- The salvor can ask for a security to be lodged that will cover his possible claims for salvage.
- The salvor will have a maritime lien on the salved ship, but he will not exercise this right provided the required security is lodged.
- Agreement and arbitration shall be governed by the law of England.

No Cure, No Pay

The term of *no cure, no pay* means that only successful salvage will be paid for though it was generally accepted that if a part of the cargo was saved, the owner would be required to pay salvage for that part.

However, with the growing concern for the environment and the damage (and cost) that pollution could inflict, oil tanker owners were aware that in a salvage situation, the salvor would not attempt anything where his expenditure of equipment and money did not produce some amount of financial return, i.e., no cure, no pay, was not the best basis on which to negotiate a contract.

In 1989, an international conference was called to consider the application of salvage and how it was to be viewed in a contemporary maritime industry with the emphasis on the safety of life, property, and the environment.

This conference has produced an international convention on salvage with far-reaching effects for the saving of property and environment.

It was decided that the reward for salvage would be fixed with a view to encouraging salvage operations and would take into account the following:

- The salved value of the ship or other property
- The skill and efforts of the salvors in preventing or minimizing damage to the environment
- The measure of success obtained by the salvor
- The nature and degree of danger
- The skill and efforts of the salvor in salving the ship, other property, and life
- The time used and expenses and losses incurred by the salvor
- The risk of liability and other risks run by the salvors and their equipment
- The promptness of the services rendered
- The availability and use of ships and other equipment intended for salvage operations
- The state of readiness and efficiency of the salvor's equipment and the value thereof (article 13)

The rewards for salvage operations cannot exceed the value of the ship or other property salved.

Special Compensation

The convention also recognizes the significance of previous LOF in that unsuccessful salvage operations do not get paid for; thus it was agreed that in cases of pollution, the salvor would receive some remuneration.

If the circumstances of the case are such that the salvor is not eligible for salvage under the rules of article 13 for a salvage operation in respect of a ship which by itself or its cargo threaten damage to the environment, he will be entitled to special compensation from the owner of the ship equivalent to his expenses.

However, if he has prevented or minimized damage to the environment, the special compensation payable maybe increased up to a maximum of 30 percent of the expenses incurred, and in very special circumstances, a tribunal may decide that the compensation may be increased further to 100 percent of the expenses incurred (article 14).

Non-salvage Operations

The above section on salvage *does not* apply to agreements voluntarily entered into

- To save property off ships that are already sunk
- To remove wrecks
- To tow ships broken down that are not in danger
- To provide harbor tugs
- To tow oil rigs or disabled ships

These shipping operations would be dealt with by normal contract law and not done in the heat of the moment.

Protest

If any incidents occur during the voyage, the master must be encouraged to note protest.

When the master of a ship "notes protest," he makes a declaration on oath, before a consular official, magistrate, or notary public that an incident occurred or that loss or damage has been or may have been caused by circumstances or actions beyond the master's control.

The sworn statement must be supported by relevant logbook entries and the evidence of other crew members.

At the time of noting protest, the master should reserve the right to extend it if and when the full extent of the loss or damage is later ascertained.

A protest should be noted as early as possible after the incident to which it relates, i.e., at the next port. When the protest concerns cargo, it should be tendered within twenty-four hours of arrival at the port and before "breaking bulk" or commencement of discharge.

Noting protest is advisable when

- Boisterous weather on passage may have caused damage to cargo
- Any *happening* has caused or may have caused damage to the ship
- Deterioration of cargo on passage is anticipated because of its condition on shipment. The bills of lading for the cargo must also have been appropriately "claused."
- Rough weather has prevented the normal cargo ventilation or bilge sounding routine being carried out, especially with perishable cargo
- The charterer or shipper is not abiding by the terms of the charter party, e.g., no cargo for shipment, undue delay in loading, cargo of a sort not allowed by the C/P, refusal to pay demurrage, and refusal to accept bills of lading after signing because of clausing by master.
- No consignee appears at the discharge port or fails to discharge cargo or pay freight according to the C/P
- A general average sacrifice or expenditure has been made.

A "happening" that caused damage to the ship could include circumstances involving other ships, e.g., collision, a foul berth or anchorage, damage in berthing and shifting berth by other vessels, improper gangway by "inside" ship, etc.

In some countries, the vessel's legal rights are not affected by the absence of a note of protest, e.g., the United Kingdom where its main function is to support the claim of a cargo owner on his insurers. However, in most other countries, the protest forms the first obligatory step in the establishment of a legal claim.

The original protest is entered in a register at the authority where it was made and certified copies are issued to the master on payment of a fee. The master should obtain three copies and send two of them to the owner/managers of the vessel and keep one on board for reference. Relevant copies of logbooks, statements of crew, and any other supporting evidence must be forwarded to the operator with the note of protest.

Sample Note of Protest

Sir,

On this day, the 22nd day of June, one thousand nine hundred and ninety-five, before me _____, Notary of the City of Riga, Latvia, Notary Public, duly admitted and sworn, personally appeared _____, the master of the motor vessel *Aco Trader* belong to the Port of Limassol of the burthen of 65,000 GRT, by measurement, or thereabouts, which sailed from Novorossiysk on or about the 5th day of June 1995 and there with to Piraeus, Glasgow, and Hamburg and arrived in this Port of Riga on the 21st day of June 1995.

It is declared that this vessel at various times on passage met moderate and rough seas and swell, pitched and rolled, shipped spray and water, and encountered rain.

And fearing damage may have been sustained by the said vessel or cargo during the said voyage, he thus enters a note of his protest hereafter to be extended in due form if necessary.

SEAL
OF   Signed..
NOTARY PUBLIC   Notary Public

              Signed..
                                          Master of *Aco Trader*

From my vast experience in the industry it's imperative to understand the multiple functions of all the operations and following their rules and regulation will keep you at your best practice.

Anytime lose is huge money spent on nothing. All shippers are always in such great position to make money on each operation when the charterer make mistake in their timing thus its usually good to make sure that all operations are pre plan and well-coordinated by a professional operator

Once there is protest from the surveyor or master to other parties this means there will be a claim at the end of the operations and in shipping the cost for simple mistake is usually huge

EPILOGUE

I'm inspired to put this piece of work together due to the following reasons.

As a young entrepreneur, especially coming from an African background where there is nothing to support such a worthy career. I came across many challenges and learned this profession the hard way.

There were no universities that offered marine courses in the region, there was no pre-knowledge of choices to become a mariner. As a young African man, I wanted to be more than a sea man. There was oceanography and seaman schools which was not publicized to young students to the maritime industry.

I grew up close to a ship channel, every day, at early hours there were ships sailing out or coming into the port and blowing their loud great horns. It became a tradition in my local community then! This is how I built my love towards this great maritime industry. Being a kid, I already knew what I wanted to become when I grew up!

After my high school years, I worked for a few maritime companies in Africa before I left Africa to study maritime courses abroad where I gained distinctive theoretical knowledge and culture of working in the maritime industry.

My love for this industry propelled me to get to where I am today. It's amazing how passion drove me to the top. I became a consultant at a very young age because I was exposed to solving major marine collusion, damages, loss adjustments, court cases, investigation etc.

For me Maritime Books are essential. I have read books from different authors about shipping, cargo, incidents, damages, management systems, and so on. I realized there was no African authors who has written any maritime books. Schools typically read books from authors from other maritime and elite nations.

I have put this piece of work together because I saw that African Mariners, who have played a very important role in the maritime industry went down the path without putting any books together for the young people to learn from their experiences. I have always wanted to make a difference especially in my beloved industry. I want to give something back to the industry that has helped me grow into who I have become today. I want to give quality knowledge to mariners and international businesses.

Most mariners retire and become helpless in their countries because they worked in the sea all their lives therefore finding it difficult to blend into society, I guess if they put some piece of their experiences on paper, it could serve them some accolades.

Most marine related crime investigators, government officers who enforce a country law, marine police and port control officers usually have no pre-knowledge of the maritime industry before they are given these jobs. In some countries, Marine crime related investigators cannot investigate clearly due to none exposure to maritime knowledge. They use response tactics and intimidation to investigate cases, using corrupt practice to frame their report against some ships and cargo. This frustrates ships and cargo owners who suffer these problems with marine crime related investigators who held ships, arrest crew members and detain cargos for no reasons in some countries.

INDEX

A

Act of God, 77
Acuerdo de Vina del Mar, 33
ad valorem freight, 106
affreightment, 2, 48, 53, 61, 164
annual freight vessel examination, 40
arbitration, 75, 94, 132, 168–69, 171
arrival, 90, 98, 102, 104, 111, 119, 126–27, 174
arrived ship, 96, 98–99, 102–3, 108, 110

B

Baltic Exchange, 56
berth, 48, 74, 97–98, 101–2
berth charter, 96, 102
bill of lading, 5, 51, 59–62, 64–68, 71–72, 74–75, 79, 81–83, 85, 105, 109, 164
bill of lading freight, 106
blockades, 101, 103, 117
broker, 4–8, 56–59, 136–37, 140
bulk carriers, 24, 49

C

cancelling clauses, 91, 109
captive insurance, 138–39
cargo exclusion, 93
cargo information, 126
cargo insurance, 139, 147
cargo interest, 5
cargo loss, 155, 157
cargo owner, 5, 8, 51, 74, 80, 105, 107, 132–33, 136–37, 139, 146, 153, 163, 168, 174
cargo superintendent, 5
cargo supernumeraries, 59
Caribbean Memorandum of Understanding, 33
carriage, 50, 52, 57, 59, 62, 71–73, 82–84, 86, 96, 126, 157
carrier, 2, 15, 60–62, 70–86, 106, 118, 151–53, 157–58, 162–64
cash flow, 42, 44–46
certificates of financial responsibility (COFR), 160
charterer, xi, 2, 5–6, 21, 51, 57–59, 63–65, 67–68, 72, 85, 87–104, 107–9, 111, 113–14, 116–19, 121–23, 126–27, 129–30, 146, 153, 157, 159, 174, 176
chartering brokers, 5, 56
charter party, 5, 55, 57, 59, 65–66, 72, 85–88, 90–94, 100, 102–3, 109–14, 117, 120–21, 125–26, 163, 174
charter party freight, 104–5
charter period, 91
clauses, 59, 65, 74, 76, 91, 94, 97, 101–2, 108–10, 112–13, 117, 121, 140–43, 163–64, 170
collision, 23, 77, 132, 134, 139, 142, 148–49, 151, 155–57, 168, 174

Convention for the Prevention of the Pollution of the Sea by Oil (OILPOL), 21
Convention for the Unification of Certain Rules of Law Respecting Assistance and Salvage at Sea, 169
Convention on Load Lines, 14
Convention on Maritime Search and Rescue (MERSAR), 23
Convention on the International Regulations for the Prevention of Collision at Sea (COLREGS), 23, 36
Convention on the Prevention of Marine Pollution by Dumping of Wastes and Other Matter, 21
Convention on Tonnage Measurement of Ships, 14
Cost, Insurance, Freight (CIF), 69–70, 155
crew, 6, 11–14, 16–17, 20, 22, 28, 33–34, 36, 38, 40, 88–89, 121, 125, 129–30, 132, 141, 148, 156, 166, 175

D

damage liens, 167–68
dead freight, 106–7, 110, 163
deadweight cargo, 97
demise charter, 87
demise charterer, 87, 120
demurrage, 110, 113–16, 122, 149, 163, 174
dispatch, 108, 110, 114–15
dock charter, 102
due diligence, 73–74, 79, 100, 117, 152, 157–59

E

environment, 14, 19, 21–22, 24, 27, 32–33, 35–36, 38–39, 150, 170–73
equitable lien, 161
expenditure, 134, 143–46, 153, 171, 174
expenditure control, 131

F

flag, 10, 12–13, 17–18, 32–33, 36, 39
flag state, 13, 22, 24, 33, 35–36, 38–39, 54
foreign merchant ships, 33
forwarding agent, 5–7, 50
Free on Board (FOB), 69
freight, 2, 5, 43, 50, 52, 57–58, 65–66, 70, 86, 90, 95, 97, 103–8, 123, 134, 146, 149, 160, 162–66, 174
freight clause, 105
freight forwarder, 2–3, 50–51, 63
freight market, 56–57
freight money, 65
freight paid, 65
freight prepaid, 65
freight rates, 4, 12, 50, 52, 57–58, 109, 122, 124
fuel, 92, 121–23, 129, 146

G

general average, 80, 105, 109, 133–35, 139, 142–47, 149, 153–54, 162–64, 174
general average contributions, 135, 146–47, 153–54, 162–64
Germany, 11, 84

goods, 2–6, 48, 60–64, 69–76, 78–86, 90, 95, 106–7, 109, 117, 131, 136, 147, 153, 158, 162–64, 168
gross tonnage, 16, 37, 148, 151

H

Hague Rules, 60–61, 71, 81, 83, 109
Hague-Visby, 61–62, 71, 81, 151–52, 158
Hague-Visby Rules (HVRs), 60–61, 71–74, 79–80, 82–84, 109, 132, 157
Hamburg Rules, 60, 62, 84, 109, 158
high-risk vessels, 37
holidays, 112–14

I

indemnity, 67, 75, 109, 148–50
independent surveyors, 7
inspection, 31–32, 34–37
institute clauses, 133, 140–41
insurance, 4, 12, 44, 46, 70–71, 125, 129–30, 134, 136–39, 141–42, 146, 155
Insurance Companies Act, 137–38
insurer, 8, 105, 134–35, 137, 140, 157, 174
International Association of Classification Societies (IACS), 9
International Bulk Chemical (IBC), 15
International Convention for Safe Containers, 23
International Convention for the Prevention of Pollution from Ships (MARPOL), 21–22, 24, 34, 36, 54
International Convention on Civil Liability for Oil Pollution, 151, 159
International Labour Organization (ILO), 12, 16, 34
International Maritime Dangerous Goods Code (IMDG), 23
International Maritime Organization (IMO), 9, 13
International Monetary Fund (IMF), 81
International Oil Pollution Prevention (IOPP), 36
International Safety Management (ISM), 23
investment, 45–46
ISM (International Safety Management), 23–25

J

jurisdiction, 12–13, 166

L

lading freight, 106
Latin American Agreement, 33
lay days, 57, 100, 112
lay time, 57, 108, 110–11, 114–15, 125
letter of indemnity (LOI), 65, 67–68
lien, 44, 66, 94, 109, 147, 154, 160–64, 167–68
liner brokers, 4
liner service, 50–52
Lloyd's Open Form (LOF), 170
Lloyd's Register of Ships, 9
Lloyd's syndicate, 137–38
loading broker, 4–5, 7, 50, 63
load lines, 14–16, 34, 36

load port, 52, 66, 98, 122, 127
London Maritime Arbitrators Association (LMAA), 94
London Market, 136
lump sum freight, 95, 97, 106

M

maintenance, 31, 44, 121, 125, 129–31
Mareva injunction, 166
marine casualties, 17, 41–42, 135
marine insurance, 4, 133–35, 137, 148
Marine Insurance Act, 133–35
marine pollution, 9, 21
Maritime Claims Convention (MCC), 152, 155–56, 158–59
maritime liens, 161, 164–68, 171
Maritime Search and Rescue (MERSAR), 23
master, 5, 18–19, 29, 34–35, 37, 63–69, 75–77, 80, 82, 95, 98–99, 101, 107–8, 117, 119, 126–28, 141–42, 145, 147, 154, 156, 158, 166–67, 169–70, 173–76
master sail, 66
master's disbursements, 165–67
merchant's broker, 5

N

Norway, 11
notice of readiness (NOR), 97

O

obligations, secondary, 100, 118
owners, 6, 10–12, 38, 45, 58, 60–61, 63–69, 72, 78, 83, 87, 91–92, 98–99, 101, 104–5, 107–9, 113–14, 120, 122, 127, 132, 135, 152, 160, 163, 171–72

P

P & I clubs, 44, 64, 67, 121, 128, 131–33, 148–50, 159, 168
Paris Memorandum of Understanding, 33
Particular average, 134
passenger ships, 6, 23–24, 53–54
pirates, 77
pollution, 13, 21, 24, 27, 34, 54, 150–52, 155, 158–59, 165, 171–72
port, 6, 12, 17, 23, 34–35, 37, 39, 52, 67–68, 72, 77, 90, 93–94, 96–98, 100–103, 106–7, 110, 112–13, 115, 117–22, 154, 174, 177
port charter, 102
Port of Limassol, 175
port of refuge, 146, 150, 154–55
Port of Riga, 175
port state control, 13, 17, 19, 33
Possessory Liens, 161–62
pro rata freight, 106
protection and indemnity associations, 148
protest, 150, 173–76

R

registration, 11–12
remuneration, 4, 89, 95, 104, 169, 171–72
respondentia, 165–66
running days, 112, 114

S

sacrifice, 134, 144–47, 153
safe berths, 118
safe port, 93, 100, 117–18
safety management certificates (SMC), 24–26, 32
Safety Management System (SMS), 25–32
Safety of Life at Sea (SOLAS), 14–15, 24, 34, 36, 54, 156
salvage, 94, 142, 165, 167, 169–73
salvage lien, 168
salvors, 170–72
seaworthiness, 73–74, 83, 92, 100
Shelltime, 88–89, 117, 126
Shellvoy, 96, 99, 108, 117
Shipboard Oil Pollution Emergency Plan (SOPEP), 22, 126
shipbrokers, 4
ship manager, 14, 52, 131, 156
ship mortgage bank, 45
shipowner's brokers, 4
shipper, xi, 1–2, 5, 8, 61–62, 66–67, 71–72, 74–75, 78, 80–86, 95, 97, 107, 123, 126, 128, 174, 176
shipping agent, 6
shipping finance, 42
standards, minimum, 16–18, 34
Standards of Training, Certification, and Watchkeeping (STCW), 16–19, 24, 34
subsidiary, 138
substandard ship, 16, 34, 38, 41
Sundays, 112, 114
surveyors, 3, 7–8, 35–36, 73, 128, 142, 150, 176
syndicates, 138, 140

T

tanker voyage chartering, 58
Tank Vessel Examination (TVE), 39
targeted classification societies, 39
targeted owner, 38–39, 41
time charter party, 51, 63, 88–90, 120, 125
time charters, 43, 45, 87, 89, 92–94, 126, 128
time clause, 97, 99, 103, 112–13
Tokyo, 33
tonnage, 16, 152
tramp operation, 52–53
Transmarine Mutual Strike Assurance Association, 149
transshipment, 65, 68

U

UN Conference on the Law of the Sea III (UNCLOS III), 21
United Kingdom, 11
United Kingdom's Carriage of Goods by Sea Act, 71
United Nations Conference on Trade and Development (UNCTAD), 12, 51, 60
United Nations Convention on Conditions, 12
United States, 11
unseaworthiness, 76, 92, 109, 157
USCG Port State Control Initiative, 37, 127
US Oil Pollution Act of 1990 (OPA), 160

V

vessel response plan (VRP), 126, 160
voyage charter parties, 53, 63, 95–97, 110, 122–23, 125

W

wages lien, 168
watchkeeping, 17
waybill, 63
working days, 86, 111–12, 114
Worldwide Tanker Nominal Freight Scale (Worldscale), 58, 95, 122

Y

York-Antwerp Rules, 133, 143

www.ingramcontent.com/pod-product-compliance
Lightning Source LLC
Chambersburg PA
CBHW030938180526
45163CB00002B/615